Branded Entertainment and Cinema

The history of Italian cinema is mostly regarded as a history of Italian auteurs. This book takes a different standpoint, looking at Italian cinema from the perspective of an unusual but influential actor: advertisers. From the iconic Vespa scooter and the many other *Made in Italy* products placed in domestic and international features, to the television programme *Carosello*'s early format of branded entertainment, up through the more recent brand-integration cases in award-winning feature films like *The Great Beauty*, the Italian film and advertising industries have frequently and significantly intersected in ways that remain largely unexplored by academic research. This book contributes to filling this gap by focusing on the economic and cultural influence that advertising and advertisers' interests have been exerting on Italian film production between the post-war period and the 2010s. Increasingly market-oriented film policies, ongoing pressure from Hollywood competition, and the abnormal economic as well as political power held by Italian ad-funded broadcasters are among the key points addressed by the book. In addition to a macro-level political-economic analysis, the book draws on exclusive interviews with film producers and promotional intermediaries to provide a meso-level analysis of the practices and professional cultures of those working at the intersection of Italian film and advertising industries.

Providing an in-depth yet clear and accessible overview of the political and economic dynamics driving the Italian media landscape towards unprecedented forms of marketisation, this book is a valuable resource for academics and students in the fields of film and media studies, marketing, advertising, and Italian studies.

Gloria Dagnino, PhD, works at the Institute of Media and Journalism of the Università della Svizzera Italian (USI), where she teaches film economics within the Master program in Film Studies of the Swiss Cinema Network. She is also the Equal Opportunities officer at USI. Her research interests include political economy of media, branded content, media diversity and Italian cinema.

Routledge Critical Advertising Studies

Routledge Critical Advertising Studies tracks the profound changes that have taken place in the field of advertising. Presenting thought-provoking scholarship from both prominent scholars and emerging researchers, these groundbreaking, short-form publications cover cutting-edge research concerns and contemporary issues within the field. Titles in the series explore emerging trends, present detailed case studies, and offer new assessments of topics such as branded content, economic surveillance, product placement, gender in marketing, and promotional screen media. Responding quickly to the latest developments in the field, the series is intellectually compelling, refreshingly open, provocative, and action-oriented.

Series Editor: Jonathan Hardy

Alternative Reality Games
Stephanie Janes

Branded Entertainment and Cinema
The Marketisation of Italian Film
Gloria Dagnino

For more information about this series, please visit: https://www.routledge.com/Routledge-Critical-Advertising-Studies/book-series/RCAS

Branded Entertainment and Cinema
The Marketisation of Italian Film

Gloria Dagnino

LONDON AND NEW YORK

First published 2020
by Routledge
2 Park Square, Milton Park, Abingdon, Oxon OX14 4RN

and by Routledge
52 Vanderbilt Avenue, New York, NY 10017

Routledge is an imprint of the Taylor & Francis Group, an informa business

© 2020 Gloria Dagnino

The right of Gloria Dagnino to be identified as author of this work has been asserted by them in accordance with sections 77 and 78 of the Copyright, Designs and Patents Act 1988.

All rights reserved. No part of this book may be reprinted or reproduced or utilised in any form or by any electronic, mechanical, or other means, now known or hereafter invented, including photocopying and recording, or in any information storage or retrieval system, without permission in writing from the publishers.

Trademark notice: Product or corporate names may be trademarks or registered trademarks, and are used only for identification and explanation without intent to infringe.

British Library Cataloguing-in-Publication Data
A catalogue record for this book is available from the British Library

Library of Congress Cataloging-in-Publication Data
Names: Dagnino, Gloria, author.
Title: Branded entertainment and cinema: the marketisation of Italian film/ Gloria Dagnino.
Description: London; New York: Routledge, 2020. | Series: Routledge critical advertising studies | Includes bibliographical references and index.
Identifiers: LCCN 2019033642 (print) | LCCN 2019033643 (ebook) | ISBN 9780815348528 (hardback) | ISBN 9781351166843 (ebook)
Subjects: LCSH: Motion picture industry–Italy–History. | Motion picture industry–Economic aspects–Italy. | Motion picture industry–Social aspects–Italy. | Motion pictures–Economic aspects–Italy. | Motion pictures–Social aspects–Italy. | Advertising–Italy–History. | Product placement in mass media–Italy–History.
Classification: LCC PN1993.5.I88 D326 2020 (print) | LCC PN1993.5.I88 (ebook) | DDC 791.430945–dc23
LC record available at https://lccn.loc.gov/2019033642
LC ebook record available at https://lccn.loc.gov/2019033643

ISBN: 978-0-8153-4852-8 (hbk)
ISBN: 978-1-351-16684-3 (ebk)

Typeset in Times New Roman
by Deanta Global Publishing Services, Chennai, India

Contents

Acknowledgements vii

Introduction 1

1 Gold, plastic, and lead: Italy between the 1950s and the 1970s 9

 1.1 Made in Italy: The manufacture of Italianness 9
 1.2 Italy and the American-style economic boom 13
 1.3 Italian television in the monopoly era 18
 1.4 Italy and the golden age of cinema 24
 Notes 32

2 The normalisation of anomaly: Italy between the 1980s and the 2000s 34

 2.1 Media, advertising, and politics: the years of convergence 34
 2.2 Politics as marketing, marketing politics 37
 2.3 It's not (only) RAI: the Italian television duopoly 44
 2.4 Italian cinema between advertising, television, and the state 52
 Notes 60

3 The imperfect marketisation: Italian advertising and cinema in the 2000s 62

 3.1 (Branded) content is king 62
 3.2 Millennium bugs: Brands and films in times of disruptions 63

vi *Contents*

3.3 Levelling the field? A new policy framework for brands and films 65

3.4 The Italian market for brands and films 71

3.5 Who serves whom? The creative impact of brands in films 77

Notes 84

4   Conclusions   **86**

A friendly separation 88
The American way 89
Advertising: What's in a name? 90
Notes 92

References   93
Index   103

Acknowledgements

I would like to thank the Italian cinema and advertising industry practitioners that have lent me generous portions of their time to discuss the topics presented in this book; their passion and professionalism, despite the many difficulties, is admirable. I thank the editorial team at Routledge, especially Jennifer Vennall, for her patience and support. I am grateful to the Swiss National Science Foundation for funding my year as visiting research fellow at the University of East London: it has been an invaluable experience, without which this book could not have been written. To my brilliant colleagues at the Institute of Media and Journalism of the Università della Svizzera italiana: thank you for believing in me and for encouraging me to do the same. For her friendship and advice, I am thankful to Fernanda Gallo, my number one source of inspiration on how to be a woman in academia. A heartfelt thank you goes to Giuseppe Richeri, Raffaele De Berti, and Jonathan Hardy for their guidance and enduring support. I thank my family—mamma, papà, Alberto, and Dada—and my chosen family—Giulia and Vanessa—for really wanting to see the end result of this research. To Elena, for being my wonderwall since the early stages of my doctoral research, when I did not know where it would have taken me: *grazie*!

Introduction

The year 2016 opened in Italy with an unprecedented cinematic sensation: the box office release of what was about to become the top-grossing Italian film of all time. This record-breaking picture was *Quo Vado?*, a comedy about a middle-aged slacker, played by popular TV comedian Checco Zalone, who goes to any length to hold on to his cushy government job. *Quo Vado?* ("Where am I going?"), an Italian spin on the Latin phrase (and arguably first cinematic blockbuster) *Quo Vadis* ("Where are you going?"), grossed over 65 million euros in the domestic market by the end of the year, thus becoming the second top-grossing film ever in Italian theatres, after James Cameron's *Avatar* (2009) (Cinetel 2016). On January 3, only two days after its theatrical release, the then Minister of Culture Dario Franceschini complimented *Quo Vado?* via Twitter by saying that the film's extraordinary success was beneficial to the Italian film sector as a whole. The film also spurred heated debate among critics, columnists, and intellectuals who commented, either positively (Minuz 2015b; Canova 2016) or negatively (Fofi 2016), about the film's socio-cultural resonance in contemporary Italy, as well as about the aggressive distribution and pricing policies that boosted the film's box office performance (Fiorelli 2016; Turrini 2016).

However remarkable, the success of *Quo Vado?* is just the most striking manifestation of a trend that has been characterising Italian cinema since the late 1970s, with increasing intensity over the last 20 years: a marked dependence on television. From a creative perspective, such dependence consists of the use of characters, situations, and storylines drawn from popular TV programmes. In fact, if we look at the top-ten-grossing Italian films of all time, we can see that all of them feature performers and characters whose popularity originated on television.[1] Since the turn of the 2000s, this trend has further intensified, as the number of Italian films starring comedians and performers "made in television" has more than tripled between 2000 and 2012 (Cucco and Scaglioni 2013). From an economic perspective, Italian cinema's dependence on television emerges in the industrial structure that enables the

2 Introduction

very production of Italian films and their access to an audience. Italy's major broadcasters—RAI, the public service broadcaster, and Mediaset, the main commercial competitor—both operate in the film sector as vertically integrated companies. At the level of film production, RAI and Mediaset operate, respectively, through the subsidiaries RAI Cinema, and Medusa and Taodue; in film distribution through 01 Distribution and Medusa; and, until few years ago, Mediaset also controlled Italy's leading film exhibition chain, The Space, which was acquired in 2014 by multinational company Vue International.

The financial contribution of RAI and Mediaset to Italian film production, mainly done through pre-sales of copyright and co-production agreements, accounts for an estimated 40–45 per cent of Italian films' production budgets (MiBACT 2016; Barra and Scaglioni 2017). Broadcasters' investment in film production is far from exceptional within the international film sector: the EU, for instance, requires broadcasters based in member states to devote at least 10 per cent of their programming budget to European works created by producers who are independent of broadcasters (see Article 17 of Directive 2010/13/EU). In Italy, though, certain peculiarities exist that make filmmakers' dependence on television money particularly critical. These peculiarities have to do with the Italian media system as a whole and can be summarised as three main, long-standing features: (1) a highly concentrated television market, (2) advertising spending abnormally skewed towards television, and (3) a subaltern relationship between politics and media. While apparently unrelated to cinema, these three aspects interplay so as to significantly affect how Italian films are conceived, financed, produced, and, ultimately, their content and aesthetics.

This book looks at the intersections and reciprocal influence existing between four major players in the Italian cultural sector: advertising, television, cinema, and the state. Such influence exerts itself as a flow of economic as well as symbolic capital that has advertising, I argue, as its catalyst. Thus, the book deconstructs and examines the role advertising has been playing in shaping a significant part of Italian screen media and culture. While scholars have extensively investigated the role of advertising in the formation of Italian culture, they have mainly done so in relation to print and broadcasting media. This book takes a step further and looks at advertising as a form of economic and cultural agency over Italian film production. Advertisers influence contemporary film production by leveraging in specific ways the corporate relations, economic power, symbolic capital, and regulatory framework that underpin their position in the Italian media system, and that derive, either directly or indirectly, from the three aforementioned peculiarities. Let us briefly present each of these (in many ways interconnected) peculiarities, and how they have been enabling advertisers to hold such a powerful and yet largely unexplored leverage over Italian film production.

Introduction 3

(1) The Italian Communications Regulatory Authority reports that in 2016 the Italian free-to-air (FTA) television market scored 3.588 points on the Herfindahl-Hirschman index that measures market concentration (AGCOM 2017). This means that the Italian television market is "highly concentrated" (Padovani 2015: 133). Scarce competition has always been a feature of the Italian television market. Earlier, this was the result of the 25-year-long monopoly of RAI, the public service broadcaster. Since the mid-1980s, the television monopoly was replaced by a duopoly, an "imperfect" one[2] (Ortoleva 2008: 98), between RAI and the commercial competitor Fininvest (rebranded Mediaset in 1993), which endures today. Since the 1980s, RAI and Fininvest/Mediaset have dominated both the television and the film market in Italy, which means that they can retain significant control over which films can be made, with what kinds of budgets, and what visibility those films can enjoy, both in theatres and in subsequent distribution windows. RAI and Mediaset have such a powerful position within the Italian film industry that for national producers it is virtually "unthinkable" (Corsi 2001: 141) to make a film without the financial participation of one of the two. Since film producers depend heavily on the backing of broadcasters, "the Italian film market appears to be mediated, as the main clients of those who make movies is another business (the broadcaster), rather than the filmgoers" (Montanari 2007: 54). This means that decisions concerning the financing and production of motion pictures are in significant measure guided by logics that pertain to the television medium, rather than cinema. To put it briefly, when broadcasters invest in film production, they are to a large extent interested with how the film will work on the small screen, whether it will fit the network's editorial line, and whether and how it will meet the needs of their stakeholders. This brings us to the second peculiarity of the Italian media market: the abnormally skewed distribution of advertising resources towards television.

(2) Advertisers are universally a major stakeholder for the broadcasting industry, but in Italy their economic influence is particularly strong. Despite the rise of digital media, Italian television still receives nearly half of the overall annual advertising expenditure: 48 per cent in 2016. As a point of comparison, in the same year, the television share of advertising expenditure was 25 per cent in Great Britain and Germany, 28 per cent in France, and 39 per cent in Spain, which also corresponds to the average share across the 28 EU countries (EAO 2017: 18). The lion's share of these investments, up to 67 per cent (R&S Mediobanca 2019), goes to Mediaset, the commercial end of the broadcasting duopoly, and also, as previously noted, a major player in the Italian film

4   *Introduction*

production and distribution market. This inevitably raises questions as to what types of cinematic productions are likely to be supported by an advertiser-funded company, with such a powerful position in both the broadcasting and the film market. Such a question is particularly apt in today's convergent media sector, where the pursuit of corporate synergies is a strategy commonly implemented by media companies worldwide (Hardy 2010, 852011). Notably, it seems crucial to examine whether and how the privileged relationship between advertisers and broadcasters, coupled with the latter's key role in the national film industry, affects Italian motion pictures from the twofold perspective of artistic and economic production. In Italy, the collaboration between advertising and television industries has been described as a "symbiotic mechanism", whereby "as years go by, one takes the features of the other" (Pitteri 2006: 172). From a creative perspective, such symbiosis can be traced back to a particular moment and event in television history: the year 1957, when the advertising programme *Carosello* (Carousel), began to air. Carosello was a 15-minute-long advertising programme broadcast daily on prime time by the then only channel available on Italian television. It consisted of four to five short comedy sketches that were paid for by advertisers. The format and contents of *Carosello* were meticulously regulated by the public service broadcaster. There were two paramount rules: the first dictated that in each sketch the entertainment bit (so-called *pezzo*) had to prevail over the proper advertising bit (so-called *codino*), and the second rule imposed that each sketch could only be aired twice. Such rules, coupled with the extensive pre-emptive censorship of any word, character, or situation even remotely at odds with a stringent Catholic morality, spurred the creation of ever more quirky solutions to bring together advertising and entertainment. Over the 20 years of its broadcasting (1957–1977), *Carosello* was actually much more akin to an entertainment programme than it was to advertising. Many *Carosello* episodes were produced in the Cinecittà Studios by the same artistic and technical talents that were creating Italy's most celebrated cinematic works, and they required TV-like budgets that were unaffordable to most Italian businesses. Moreover, *Carosello* came to be perceived by the Italian audience as a genuine entertainment show, which, over time, became part of every TV-owning family's daily routine.[3] Such perception was encouraged by advertisers themselves, who bought spaces in RAI's listing magazine, *Radiocorriere*, to advertise their paid-for upcoming instalment of *Carosello*, just like it was done for regular television dramas (Dorfles 1998). In this sense, *Carosello* can be considered as an early, and particularly successful, example of what is now known as

Introduction 5

branded entertainment. One fact about *Carosello* that all media scholars and commentators agree on is that it had a profound impact on the language, topoi, and style not only of subsequent commercial communications, but of television and of all Italian screen media. Some have gone as far as to argue that, through *Carosello*, advertising has become the one driving force behind the shaping of Italy's cultural industry and collective imagination (see Pitteri 2006).

While the creative influence of advertising on the Italian mediascape started as soon as the public service channel started to broadcast it, its ability to steer economic resources towards television boomed in the 1980s, with the launch and rapid consolidation of nationwide commercial networks. Indeed, with the consolidation on the market of Berlusconi's three channels, advertisers' investments grew unprecedentedly. In 1980, television accounted for 25.7 per cent of the overall Italian advertising expenditure; four years later, when Silvio Berlusconi acquired his third channel, that figure exceeded 47 per cent, which is television's advertising share still today (Brigida et al. 2004: 26). The steep growth of Fininvest channels through the 1980s was due to Berlusconi's innovative and aggressive strategy: in terms of business management (e.g. by marketing to small enterprises) and in terms of content programming (e.g. by recruiting celebrities until then strongly associated with the public service broadcaster). Berlusconi's media venture, though, could not have thrived had he not benefited from a favourable political climate, which, for many years, did not stop, and then ultimately legitimised an entrepreneurial boom built in violation of a number of juridical decisions. This brings us to the third peculiarity that we need to address in relation to the Italian media system, namely the subaltern relationship the media system has with political power.

(3) In April 1986, American leading entertainment trade magazine *Variety* published an article enthusiastically titled "Italy and Silvio Berlusconi invented commercial television on the European continent" (quoted in Mattelart 1991: 102). The impressive take-off of Berlusconi's commercial enterprise was in fact unprecedented in the European mediascape, which was still largely shaped by the tradition of public service broadcasting. Berlusconi's undisputable entrepreneurial ability, though, did also benefit from political connections with then Prime Minister Bettino Craxi, leader of the Italian Socialist Party which ran the country from 1983 to 1987. The Craxi executive issued a number of temporary acts, collectively dubbed "Berlusconi decree", that allowed Berlusconi's channels to stay on the air, however in violation of a number of previous juridical decisions. Between the mid-1980s and early 1990s, Berlusconi was able to build his media empire thanks to propitious

6 Introduction

political interventions, followed by a prolonged regulatory vacuum, and finally by a broadcasting law that legalised *ex post facto* his position in the market. In 1994, when Berlusconi himself entered politics, the conflict of interest between his private media enterprises and his public role exploded for the first time, only to reappear at each of his subsequent prime minister electoral victories (four over 15 years).

While Berlusconi's case represents the epitome of the intertwined relationship between media and politics in Italy, such phenomenon did not start with him, nor with commercial television. Since its inception, RAI, the public service broadcaster, operated under exclusive licence by the Italian government, which appointed executives and dictated the editorial line. This, as we shall see, had profound consequences in terms of agenda setting, freedom of expression, and political and cultural censorship, especially because Italy's government was led uninterruptedly by one party, the Christian Democrats, for 35 years. In 1975, a broadcasting reform law, aimed at making the public service broadcaster more independent and pluralistic, removed RAI from direct control of the government and put it under that of the Parliament. The result of this change was the creation of the system of *lottizzazione*, i.e. the "formalized carve-up of RAI by political parties" (Hibberd 2008: 76). According to the logic of lottizzazione, "pluralism was finally reached once each of the three main parties was able to exercise hegemony over its own broadcasting channel" (Padovani 2005: 7).

Thus, either by means of direct monopoly control, and later of the system of lottizzazione, or on the grounds of corporate ownership, Italian political forces have been exerting control over both the public service broadcaster and the leading commercial competitor. Besides obvious, detrimental effects in terms of media freedom and pluralism, this also bears consequences for the film industry, given the centrality of RAI and Mediaset in financing, producing, and distributing Italian films. Moreover, the influence of political forces, and notably that of the governing parties, on Italian cinema manifests itself, at a broader level, in the implementation of increasingly market-oriented film policies, the legalisation of product placement, and the introduction of tax incentives for consumer companies that invest in national film production.

This book explores and critically examines the increasingly central role that advertising and advertisers' interests have been playing in the Italian film industry. To examine this, we need to look at a broader picture, which includes not only the economic and regulatory development of Italian cinema, but also the evolution of consumer culture and of another major medium of popular entertainment in Italy, television. This book does not aim to provide an exhaustive treatment of all the individual themes presented so far, as to do so would require an entire library. Instead, it aims to highlight an underlying

Introduction 7

trend that has gone through the evolution of Italian cinema and audiovisual media from the post-war period up to the present day. This trend concerns the increasingly pervasive and established role that advertising has played, as an economic, aesthetic, and cultural force, in Italian film production.

The book is structured as follows: Chapters 1 and 2 provide a chronological account of the main developments undergone by the three different, but interconnected sectors of Italian society—Italian television and Italian cinema with regard to their relation to advertising. Chapter 1 focuses on the time span that goes from the early 1950s to the late 1970s, whereas Chapter 2 covers the 1980s, 1990s, and 2000s. Overall, this half-century saw massive and increasingly accelerated changes at all levels of the Italian social, economic, and cultural life. Italian advertisers and filmmakers played essential roles in such changes, sometimes to prompt them and sometimes to incorporate and mirror them in their creative works. Following the implementation of dedicated policies since the early 2000s, exchanges and collaborations between Italian advertisers and filmmakers have become increasingly frequent, but no less problematic. Chapter 3 looks at the practices that best exemplify such collaborations: product placement, tax credit for non-audiovisual companies, and branded entertainment. Such practices also illustrate very well the criticalities that the collaborations between consumer and film companies involve on both sides. The section firstly provides an overview of Italy's contemporary market for product placement, tax credit, and branded entertainment involving films: the regulatory framework and the main market players, as well as the predominant modes of their collaborations, with particular attention to the crucial role played by promotional intermediaries. To do so, the chapter relies on first-hand data and knowledge that high-profile practitioners in the Italian film and advertising sectors have generously agreed to share with the author of the book. Their identities have been concealed to protect the confidential and sometimes sensitive nature of the information they shared. Finally, a conclusive section concisely discusses three main patterns of continuity that will emerge throughout the book and highlights some important implications for future studies in critical film and advertising industries.

Notes

1 Top ten grossing Italian films of all times and respective performers from television: (1) *Quo vado?* (2016; Checco Zalone), (2) *Sole a catinelle* (2013; Checco Zalone), (3) *La vita è bella* (1997; Roberto Benigni), (4) *Che bella giornata* (2011; Checco Zalone), (5) *Benvenuti al Sud* (2010; Claudio Bisio, Alessandro Siani), (6) *Chiedimi se sono felice* (2000; Aldo, Giovanni & Giacomo), (7) *Natale sul Nilo* (2002; Fichi d'India, Biagio Izzo), (8) *Il ciclone* (1996; Leonardo Pieraccioni, Massimo Ceccherini), (9) *Benvenuti al Nord* (2012; Claudio Bisio,

8 *Introduction*

Alessandro Siani), (10) *Pinocchio* (2002; Roberto Benigni). Source: Cinetel and Movieplayer.

2 Ortoleva defines the 1980s television duopoly "imperfect" for two main reasons, both of which will be addressed in further detail over the course of the book. Firstly, because RAI and Mediaset, while being by far the biggest, were not the only nationwide players in the broadcasting market. Secondly, because the prolonged lack of clear and fair rules prevented the establishment of a level playing field in the Italian broadcasting market for at least a decade.

3 The phrase "After *Carosello*, off to bed!" (*Dopo Carosello, tutti a nanna!*) became a popular refrain that Italian parents told their children (Dorfles 1998: 91).

1 Gold, plastic, and lead
Italy between the 1950s and the 1970s

1.1 Made in Italy: The manufacture of Italianness

The concept of Italy as a territorial and cultural unity can be traced back to as early as the Roman Empire, but it only became a tangible political objective in the 19th century, during the turbulent, and continually debated, period known as the *Risorgimento* ("Resurgence"). During the sixty years following the Congress of Vienna (1814–1815), a series of military events, and notably the three wars against the occupying Austrian Empire (1848–1866), Giuseppe Garibaldi's Expedition of the Thousand (1860), and the Capture of Rome (1870), led Italy to unification as an independent nation-state, with territorial borders similar to those of today.[1] The official date of the unification is March 17, 1861, when a Kingdom of Italy was declared and Vittorio Emanuele II of Piedmont became its first king. That historical moment is considered to be the date of birth of Italy as a nation-state, but merely a first step towards the formation of an Italian national identity. Following unification, statesman and writer Massimo D'Azeglio famously stated: "We have made Italy, now we must make Italians" (*Fatta l'Italia, bisogna fare gli Italiani*). Indeed, long after becoming a unified political entity, Italy remained a patchwork of linguistic and cultural differences, where the concept of a national identity, or, to draw from Benedict Anderson's (1983) conceptualisation, of a nation-based "imagined community", was simply ignored. Rather, people would identify with the local and, interestingly, the international level. This came as the result of the Italian diaspora at the turn of the 19th and 20th century, when virtually all Italian families, especially from the Southern regions, had at least one relative relocated overseas. Therefore, as Italian sociologist Francesco Alberoni wrote:

> For decades, the United States, Brazil, Argentina were closer to many South Italian citizens than (*Central and Northern cities such as*) Viterbo, Siena, Bologna or Padua (…) Between these two poles, one

10 *Gold, plastic, and lead*

particularistic and private, made of affective bonds and immediate interests, whereas the other universalistic, abstract, international, there was a cultural void.

(Alberoni 1968: 26, my translation)

The three decades to which this chapter is devoted (1950s, 1960s, 1970s) are largely considered to be the time span when D'Azeglio's statement was finally fulfilled, and Italy reached cultural unification, long after the political one. What made it possible to fill the nation's cultural void, nearly a century after the official unification, were mass media.

Scholars agree on the "uncontentious" role (Schlesinger 1991: 298) that media play in the formation of national identities. Such role is officially acknowledged by national governments that issue public funding, tax incentives, and other protectionist measures to support mass media—and especially the film industry—in their promotion of a nation's cultural specificity. In the long aftermath of World War II, the starting period of this book, Italian people drew a sense of who they were, mostly from what they were *seeing*, rather than *reading*, on mass media. In other words, Italianness was "a system of representation" (Girelli 2009: 9) of selected notions and symbols about Italy and its people, which was primarily produced and received through visual media.[2] The foremost reason for this is the fact that in the early 1950s some 13 to 14 per cent of adults were illiterate (ISTAT 1951), with the highest concentrations being in rural and Southern areas; in the UK, by comparison, it was 1 to 2 per cent (UNESCO 1957). According to the 1951 general population census, nearly two thirds of Italians were speaking, on a daily basis, only their regional dialects, as opposed to the official Italian language (De Mauro 1968: 252). Moreover, in the same period, only 18 per cent of Italian school-aged children were enrolled in a post-primary school (De Mauro 1968: 262). In fact, Italians' limited familiarity with print culture has continued long after the implementation of mass education and the decrease of illiteracy rates to the point of becoming a defining feature of Italy in the 20th century: "Italy has been characterised this century in its forms of modern popular culture by a marked predominance of non-print culture (visual, spoken, musical) over print" (Forgacs 1990: 25–26). Visual media, in particular, have been investigated by cultural historians for their role as a vehicle for the construction and circulation of national identity in post-war Italy. Works on such topics include extensive ethnographic studies on the consumption of motion pictures (Forgacs and Gundle 2007) and television programmes (Fanchi 2002), as well as illustrated magazines (Gundle 1986). Such works inform the discourse carried on in this chapter, which looks at the intersection of advertising, cinema, and television in Italy between the 1950s and 1970s.

Gold, plastic, and lead   11

Over these decades, advertising and commercial contents were decisive in influencing what Italians got to see and appreciate on screen, including a sense of their shared identity. This was due to the political economy of film and television industries, over which advertisers exercised strong agency, as this chapter examines. At the same time, though, it was also the result of the broader cultural and ideological climate that dominated Italy since the end of World War II. After two decades of Fascist dictatorship, five years of world war, and civil conflicts between partisans and supporters of the regime, Italy was a country ravaged by poverty, inflation, and lack of public and industrial infrastructures, as well as socially and ideologically divided. In such context, and because of its strategic positioning at the crossroads between Western and Eastern Europe, post-war Italy became a crucial setting in the Cold War between American and Soviet forces for the imposition of political, ideological, and cultural hegemony over the country. The US, in particular, besides providing Italy with substantial economic aids through the European Recovery Programme (commonly known as Marshall Plan), laid out a comprehensive strategy to achieve a "cultural hegemony" (Ellwood and Kroes 1994). This way, the US aimed to detach Italy from the USSR's sphere of cultural influence, thus creating fertile ground for the political defeat of the Italian Communist Party. The cultural warfare between the US and USSR has been said to be fought "between Hollywood and Moscow" (Gundle 2000), since American cinema had an essential part in it, and in shaping the collective identity of the then newly formed Italian Republic. The cornerstone of such propaganda was the promotion of an American-style consumerism in what had traditionally been a "low consumption society" (Segreto 2002). Consumer products such as household appliances, industrial food, and toiletries became the symbols of an unprecedentedly affluent lifestyle that Italians came to know and desire, firstly, via Hollywood, and then through the imagery created by national television.

In Italy, though, secular, American-style consumerism was filtered through the lens (and censorship policies) of the Christian Democracy Party (*Democrazia Cristiana*), which led the government since 1946. The Christian Democracy, whilst "prepared to accept the process of Americanisation on a consumerist level, on a cultural level it had to find an alternative, if it was to maintain the support of the Catholic Church hierarchy" (Treveri Gennari 2009: 6). During the period covered by this chapter, the conflict between these two cultural and ideological forces had repercussions, especially, though not exclusively, for the television medium, which was under direct governance of the ruling party. The unique format of *Carosello*, the first advertising programme of Italian television, with its overly detailed rules to ensure the predominance of entertainment over commercial contents, is a striking example of what the compromise between those conflicting views

12   *Gold, plastic, and lead*

meant for Italian media. The contents of *Carosello*, and of screen-based media more generally, also reflected that twofold cultural influence. Being Italian came to be represented on screen as a unique blend of symbols and behaviours that referred, on the one hand, to consumption and consumerism, and on the other hand, to the frugal life; to an individualistic versus a more collectivist view of social life; to a modernist outlook on society, on one side, and to a vision rooted in traditions, on the other; and to secular America as well as to Catholic Italy.

Such trends influenced the notion of Italianness that national cinema and television promoted since the 1950s, by shaping it into a twofold concept: at once domestic and outward looking. With respect to domestic audiences, Italianness helped to popularise the official national language and provided a shared imagery of characters, situations, and symbols with which every Italian citizen was to identify. With respect to (primarily) international audiences, it encapsulated a set of desirable, exotic, and yet unthreatening features and values such as picturesque natural landscapes; curvaceous women and manly men; a love for genuine food and convivial eating; and, overall, a certain epicurean, care-free lifestyle. These connotations of *Italianness* were linked to the display of certain consumer products. In the case of the domestic audience, products like Vidal bath soap or Ava laundry powder, advertised in popular episodes of *Carosello*, were both the symbols of and the instruments enabling Italians to embrace the new capitalist way of life. In the case of the international audience, Italianness mainly functioned as a selling point for the new products of *Made in Italy*, such as the Vespa motorbike, manufactured by Piaggio and sold since 1946, and its integration in the American romantic comedy film *Roman Holiday* (dir. William Wyler, 1953).

The remainder of this chapter will explore in further detail the themes mentioned so far. It will do so by looking at the evolution of advertising and consumer culture, cinema, and television industries, and how these four interplayed against the changing backdrop of Italian politics, culture, and society between the 1950s and 1970s. The title of this chapter references the three materials that came to symbolically identify the time span in question. Firstly, there is the *gold* of the many "golden ages" that characterised Italian culture and society between the 1950s and 1970s: a "golden age of capitalism" (Marglin and Schor 1990), epitomised by the arrival of large-scale retail distribution, but also a "golden age of Italian cinema" (Bondanella and Pacchioni 2017: 271), which saw the maturity of great Italian directors such as Fellini, Visconti, and Antonioni, as well as the rise of a new wave of auteurs, like Bertolucci, Scola, and Moretti; *plastic*, as plastic objects began to be industrially mass produced at the end of the 1950s and soon became the symbol of Italy's economic boom and 1960s' consumerism;

Gold, plastic, and lead   13

lead, as in the "Years of Lead" (*Anni di piombo*) (late 1960s–late 1970s), a time marked by killings, abductions, and dramatic social turmoil caused by far-right and far-left terrorist organisations, which coincided with the first international oil crisis, and consequent economic austerity, and later with the end of the public service broadcaster's monopoly.

1.2 Italy and the American-style economic boom

In one of the funniest, and most iconic, scenes in Italian film history, twenty-something Nando Meliconi, played by the famous actor Alberto Sordi, scornfully rejects the plate of spaghetti and the straw-clad wine flask his mother left for him to eat late at night and instead makes himself a plate of "healthy, nutritious food" in (self-proclaimed) American style. One bite of the uninviting mixture of bread, milk, jam, yoghurt, and mustard is enough for him to give up that exotic "junk" (*zozzeria*) in favour of the more familiar pasta bowl. The film is *An American in Rome* (dir. Steno, 1954) and it tells the story of an Italian guy from a lower-middle-class family in Rome who dreams of moving to the US and is obsessed with American culture, which he tries to replicate in his everyday life: Nando always wears jeans, a cowboy belt, and a baseball cap; he rides a Harley Davidson; has the walls of his room covered with pictures of Hollywood celebrities; and speaks Italian with what he considers to be an American accent (to the comic despair of his loved ones). The film, which can be viewed as a precursor of the successful genre of *commedia all'Italiana* (Italian-style comedy), exposes with bitter irony the Americanisation trend that invested Italian culture and society in the early 1950s. The post-war Americanisation of Italy was the result of a multifaceted political strategy that comprised economic, industrial, and cultural operations. The economic aids provided under the umbrella of the Marshall Plan were essential in allowing Italy to overcome the famine and poverty afflicting the country in the aftermath of World War II. By supporting economic recovery, the US also created the ground for American companies to expand their operations into an attractive and yet unexplored market. At the same time, the Marshall Plan ran at the symbolic level, by exporting films and other cultural products that promoted American-friendly values to the Italian audience. Overall, as David Ellwood (1992: 89) wrote, the political goal of the US was to create "an economic 'United States of Europe' (...), in which the American dream could be dreamt without leaving home: 'You too can be like us!' that was the promise of the Marshall Plan". In Europe, the effects of the Marshall Plan were especially powerful on the nations that came out defeated from the war: between 1950 and 1973 Italy and Germany saw an average annual economic growth of 5 per cent, much higher than the European average

14   *Gold, plastic, and lead*

(Scarpellini 2011). In Italy, in particular, the investments made to kick-start the post-war industrial and infrastructure reconstruction, boosted economic production to a degree that was, and still is, unmatched in national history: it was the so-called "Italian economic miracle".

Consuming the miracle

The decade between mid-1950s and 1960s, and especially the 1958–1963 "boom years", came to be known as the period of the Italian economic miracle: domestic GDP was growing an impressive 6.3 per cent annually, and industrial growth rates reached more than 8 per cent per year. The miracle, however, affected Italian society unevenly: growth was predominantly concentrated in the North, and notably in the so-called industrial triangle formed by the cities of Genoa, Turin, and Milan. As a result, hundreds of thousands of people left the Southern and rural regions to relocate, often to precarious living conditions, to the outskirts of urban industrial areas.[3] Economic growth did not necessarily translate into increased wages, but it did mean the transformation of many seasonal and occasional jobs into permanent ones. This allowed young couples especially to aspire to and to plan for a more affluent life, starting from the milestone of owning their own house. These were also the years of a demographic baby boom that found no equivalent in subsequent times. Family and social life changed profoundly, compared to the largely agricultural, pre-industrial, pre-urban conditions that dominated the country before the 1950s. There were more goods on sale, more money to buy them, and more free time to enjoy them. Consumer spending grew at a higher rate than incomes (Scarpellini 2004). As Emanuela Scarpellini (2011: 129) put it: "In the Italy of the economic miracle the time had come to 'buy' happiness". Food purchases increased and diversified: consumption of meat, especially beef and veal, increased 165 per cent between 1951 and 1980, whereas consumption of sugar, an absolute luxury during wartime, tripled from post-war to 1970. At the same time, consumption of pasta remained stable, but now it could be conveniently purchased dried in industrially produced packages. Moreover, the economic miracle brought a democratisation of previously unaffordable luxury goods that, thanks to the regularisation of employment, Italians could now buy in instalments. Furnishings and transport and communications are the commodities that enjoyed the highest rates of consumption growth, respectively +89 per cent and +95 per cent from 1951 to 1970 (Scarpellini 2011: 144). Increased purchases of cars, furniture pieces, televisions, and electrical appliances speak to the reconfiguration of Italian families as more private, inward-looking, and autonomous units compared to the more collectivist and interdependent households of rural society.

Gold, plastic, and lead 15

One commodity in particular became the symbol of Italy's new material culture: the motorcycle. In 1946, the Tuscany-based motor manufacturer Piaggio launched Vespa ("wasp"), a small motorcycle with an ample front bodywork that protected the driver from dirt and allowed comfortable riding for two passengers. The first model was sold at the relatively affordable price of 80 thousand liras and production rapidly doubled from 1 million pieces in 1956 to 2 million in 1960. In 1947, Milan-based company Innocenti launched a similar scooter, Lambretta, which was cheaper and slimmer than its competitor, and was advertised with "American style slogans" (Scarpellini 2011: 143). Whilst cars were purchased by middle-class families, Vespa and Lambretta were mainly chosen by younger generations as symbols of freedom and transgression, both in Italy and abroad. In the UK, for example, Vespa and Lambretta were the transport of choice of the mod subculture that spread in London in the 1960s. Vespa and Lambretta are only the most popular examples of an array of original products designed and mass-produced by Italian manufacturers during the economic boom years. A less iconic, but equally revolutionary product that came on the market in the late 1950s was Moplen. Moplen, produced by the Italian quasi-monopolistic chemical company Montecatini, was the trademark of a polypropylene plastic material that earned its inventor, Italian chemist Giulio Natta, the Nobel Prize in 1963. Moplen's lightness and durability were advertised in some of the most memorable episodes of *Carosello*, which featured beloved TV comedian Gino Bramieri and the catchy slogan "*Mo... mo ... mo ... Moplen!*" ("Now ... now ... now ... Moplen!"). Plastic took the place of traditional materials, such as wood, metal, and glass, in the production of a variety of household products, from tableware and kitchenware to furniture pieces and children's toys. Moreover, Moplen and soon later Swedish patent Tetra Pak were employed for packaging detergents and consumables, and for safely storing them for longer periods of time. Such use proved particularly important when large-scale retail distribution arrived in Italy in the second half of the 1950s.

The first supermarket was established in Milan in 1957 upon the initiative of US industrial group International Basic Economy Corporation (IBEC). IBEC was founded in 1946 by US businessman and politician Nelson Rockefeller with the explicit goal of exporting the American business and social model to underdeveloped countries, so as to distance them from the political influence of communist Soviet Union. The company, named Supermarkets Italiani SpA, was owned 51 per cent by IBEC, while the remaining shares were controlled by a number of Italian shareholders, among which there were also the owners of *Corriere della sera*, Italy's leading newspaper (Scarpellini 2004). The arrival of American-style supermarkets disrupted the traditionally fragmented local retailing system and

16   *Gold, plastic, and lead*

brought profound changes to the Italian consumer culture, as well as industrial strategies. Shopping became primarily a self-service experience, which pushed consumer companies to shift their focus from a product to a market-oriented strategy (Scarpellini 2011). Marketing gained unprecedented importance, and the US were world leaders in that field.

Advertising modernity

Italy's first advertising agency was established in 1863 by pharmacist Attilio Manzoni in Milan, which has ever since been the national hub for the advertising sector (Codeluppi 2013). Advertising then became the site for new forms of creative expression, as important painters and visual artists of the Italian modernist avant-garde, such as Fortunato Depero, Mario Sironi, and Lucio Fontana, created print and outdoor posters campaigns for national brands like Fiat, Campari, Buitoni, and San Pellegrino. Prior to the end of World War II, Italian advertising firms mostly resembled artisan workshops, where the artist's insight and creativity prevailed in driving the advertiser's decisions. Things started to change as a result of the advent of major US and UK operators in the post-war period, and notably between 1948 and 1952. As Pitteri (2006) observed, in those "pre-miracle" years, the massive arrival of Anglo-American firms was not so much motivated by the still fragile status of Italian economy as it was by the political will to promote American values to a former enemy country. Unsurprisingly, one of the first foreign advertising agencies to open an Italian branch was J. Walter Thompson, which was entrusted with public relations for the Marshall Plan.[4] Soon after, all major US and UK ad agencies followed: Lever International Advertising Service (LINTAS), C.P.V., McCann Erikson, and Young & Rubicam (Segreto 2002).

Anglo-American agencies introduced new techniques and methods, like large sample polls, focus groups, psychological research, and overall a rationalised approach to market research. Moreover, foreign agencies were structured as integrated organisations that incorporated all the services a client needed: from market research to creative design; from budget management to strategic planning; from media buying to production. Such an industrial model was not dissimilar to the one that characterised (and pushed the success of) the Hollywood film industry. While the US advertising and film industries were built around a relatively few big and integrated players, in Italy both advertising and film companies were fragmented, small in size, and non-integrated. In the case of film companies, such a lighter, flexible industrial structure allowed Italian firms to be more resilient during time of economic recession, but it did also limit growth and constituted a weakness that still hinders the Italian film industry to this day. In the case of advertising

Gold, plastic, and lead 17

agencies, the arrival of big international players meant the demise of many Italian firms, which could not provide the same all-round service as integrated operators (Segreto 2002). This started a long, uninterrupted trend that led Italy's advertising market to be progressively concentrated under the control of a handful of international holdings (AGCOM 2012).

In the post-war years, Italian advertising began to develop as a modern industry. Trade bodies were established, which represented the interests of all the main advertising players: from advertising agencies, associated since 1947 in the FIP (*Federazione Italiana della Pubblicità*, "Italian Federation of Advertising"), to advertisers, represented by UPA (*Utenti Pubblicità Associati*, "Association of Advertising Users") since 1949. In the 1960s, all the major trade bodies collaborated to create the first comprehensive Advertising Code of Conduct (*Codice di autodisciplina pubblicitaria*), which entered into force in 1966. Advertising investments more than tripled, from 25 billion liras in 1950 to 90 billion in 1960, spurred firstly by the economic boom, then by the spread of television broadcasting (Segreto 2002: 19).

At the turn of the 1970s, though, advertising investments in Italy hit a decline, which became particularly noticeable between 1973 and 1974: –9 per cent, and again –3.6 per cent the following year (Brigida, Baudi Di Vesme, and Francia 2004: 20). This was largely due to the global economic crisis that hit Western societies as a result of the oil embargo decided in October 1973 by the Organization of Arab Petroleum Exporting Countries (OAPEC) countries. As a US-allied country, Italy was also struck by a severe oil shortage, which brought the government to impose a series of measures, including a ban on the circulation of motor vehicles on non-working days and the reduction of public lighting to reduce energy consumption. The trend in advertising investments continued to be uneven throughout the decade. In addition to the economic uncertainty due to the global oil crisis, there was the Italian social and political situation which was marked by severe tensions and divisions. The years between 1969 and 1980 in Italy were named "Years of Lead" because of the armed struggle that far-right and far-left extra-parliamentary groups carried out in the country over that period. Italy was struck by dozens of politically motivated attacks, which culminated in the tragic events of 1978 and 1980. In March 1978, the left-wing terrorist organisation Red Brigades kidnapped and subsequently killed Aldo Moro, then president of the Christian Democracy Party, and his bodyguards. On August 2, 1980, far-right extremists placed a bomb in the waiting room of Bologna main train station, at the time crowded with travellers leaving for summer holidays, which exploded and killed 85 people. The Bologna massacre was the bloodiest terrorist act of Italy's post-war history and is considered to be the closing act of the Years of Lead.[5] Over this period, advertisers adjusted their communication, lowering budget

18 *Gold, plastic, and lead*

and opting for sober messages, which resonated better with the climate of economic austerity and social turmoil in the country.

Even from this concise overview, one can appreciate how significantly, as well as rapidly, Italian society has changed in the space of 30 years. The economic miracle, the wider access to education, and the progressive secularisation all contributed to determine a profound shift in the values underpinning Italian society. These values were no longer embodied by the rural, pre-industrial society, but by the ever-broader urban middle class. What occurred between the 1950s and 1970s was a proper "anthropological revolution" (Pasolini 1975: 50), which had consumption and consumer culture at its core. Mass media, and notably television, played a major part in this revolution, as we will see in the following pages.

1.3 Italian television in the monopoly era

Television broadcasting in Italy officially started on January 3, 1954, when presenter Fulvia Colombo concisely announced the start of the regular television service and went on listing the upcoming programmes of the day. The announcement was transmitted live from Milan, but the broadcaster also had production studios in the cities of Turin and Rome. The launch of Italian television was coeval to that of other Mediterranean countries, but it was significantly delayed in comparison to other Central and Northern European countries, which had already begun regular services in the mid-1930s.[6] Italian television started as a public service monopoly run by RAI (*Radiotelevisione italiana*, "Italian Radio-Television"). The Italian government, and notably the Ministry of Communications, granted RAI exclusive rights to nationwide television broadcasting on the basis of a renewable agreement, initially in force from 1952 to 1975. In return for exclusive rights, RAI had to comply with a set of rules and fulfil specific public interest goals, which were, and still are, listed in a "service contract" (*contratto di servizio*) signed by the broadcaster and the government. In creating the service contract, the Italian government drew inspiration from the UK model, notably from the Royal Charter and Agreement that regulates the mandate between the British government and the BBC. However, a significant difference existed between the British and the Italian systems of public service broadcasting: the Italian government, namely the Ministry of Economy and Finance, was, and still is, RAI's majority stakeholder. Thus, unlike the BBC, RAI was not only licensed, but directly controlled by the political forces that ruled the country. In the following sections we will look at some of the effects that such a politicised governance had over the first two decades of Italian public service broadcasting: effects in terms of RAI's editorial policy, as well as

Gold, plastic, and lead 19

its relation to television advertising, which, unlike the BBC, was incorporated as a source of funding since the beginning.

Mamma RAI!

Like the broader European tradition of public service television, RAI's editorial policy was primarily characterised by a strong pedagogic remit (Bourdon 2001) which applied to all the genres that made up the programming offered by the one and (for six years) only television channel. On the one hand, RAI enacted such remit through educational programmes designed and produced in collaboration with the Italian Ministry of Education. Two of them, in particular, had a substantial impact on Italian society: *Non è mai troppo tardi* ("It's never too late") and *Telescuola* ("Teleschool"). The former, which aired between 1960 and 1968, was set as a classroom, where the presenter, educator, and national treasure Alberto Manzi helped illiterate adults to learn the basics of Italian grammar, reading, and writing. *Telescuola*, which aired from 1958 to 1966, functioned as a proper televised night school, with classes on all subjects. Students, i.e. viewers, who successfully passed a final test in front of a special commission earned a real middle school degree. Such initiatives speak to the power that television had, since very soon after its launch, to reach the Italian population in a capillary way and to arrive where not even the infrastructures of public education had arrived. Besides educational programmes, RAI pursued its pedagogic remit through entertainment programming offer that championed erudition. In this regard, quiz shows were the most popular examples: unmissable weekly programmes like *Il musichiere* ("The music maker", 1957–1960), *Campanile sera* ("It's a knockout", 1959–1962), and, above all, *Lascia o Raddoppia* ("Leave it or double it", 1955–1959; the Italian version of the American show *The $64,000 Question*) were based on the contestants' deep knowledge of one or multiple subjects. RAI's pedagogic efforts and its ability to educate and create a sense of national collectiveness earned the Italian public service broadcaster the nickname "Mamma RAI" ("Mum RAI"). This nickname had both an affectionate and a sneering connotation, as it referenced the predominant tone used by the broadcaster to address its viewers: at the same time caring and condescending.

The motherly, or rather paternalistic, attitude that RAI displayed towards its audience mirrored the one that the Christian Democrat government had towards Italian voters. Mamma RAI had always successfully influenced the outcomes of political elections through news and information programming that favoured the Christian Democracy Party by silencing political opponents. Starting in the 1960s, though, Italian society grew more affluent and exigent also with regard to cultural consumption. In response to

20   *Gold, plastic, and lead*

the evolving socio-cultural climate, RAI tried to expand and diversify its offer by launching, in 1961, a second channel which was supposed to provide less traditionalist, more youth-friendly programming. The same year, the government appointed a new director general, Ettore Bernabei, and entrusted him with the task of modernising RAI, while still pushing the Christian Democrat agenda. Bernabei understood that RAI had to move beyond its pedagogic remit if it wanted to stay relevant and influential to the more progressive audience of 1960s Italy. Over this decade, RAI increased its programming offer, quantitatively and qualitatively, mostly by investing in light entertainment programmes: quiz shows; variety shows; and notably studio dramas, based on the classics (e.g. *The Odyssey*), on biopics (*Life of Dante, Saint Francis of Assisi*) and on genre literature (*The Adventure of Sherlock Holmes, Maigret*). In terms of political pluralism, though, the launch of the second channel did not really improve RAI's record, but in fact reinforced the broadcaster's reputation as a "factory of political consensus" (*fabbrica del consenso*) (Monteleone 1992: 335).

At the end of the decade, in the midst of the workers', students', and women's movements, the gap between the progressive demands coming from large parts of the Italian society, the government's hesitancy in hearing them, and the conservative ways in which the public service broadcaster reported about it, became apparent. As Scotto Lavina (2015: 67) observed, RAI did not have "the ability to interpret the generational and emotional dynamics, on top of political ones, that were setting the Italian society in motion". But it was in 1974 that the social and political gap between the public service broadcaster and Italian society broke out more dramatically during the campaign that preceded the referendum to repeal the law allowing divorce. Divorce in Italy had only been legal for four years when the Christian Democracy Party called for a popular vote to abolish it. RAI deployed a powerful propaganda campaign in favour of the abrogative vote, but its position was eventually defeated, and divorce remained legal. In the wake of the vote, Ettore Bernabei, director general for 14 years and Christian Democrat affiliate, left RAI on the eve of the first comprehensive television reform law since its inception. The 1975 broadcasting reform law introduced two main changes: (1) it established the creation of a third channel, based on regional production centres, which started transmissions at the end of 1979; and (2) removed RAI from the control of the government and put it under that of Parliament. This latter decision should have guaranteed more political independence and editorial freedom to Italian television. In fact, however, it laid the ground for the spoils system known as *lottizzazione*. From then on, an unwritten, but always respected, rule imposed that the direction of the first, and typically highest rating, channel (RAI 1) was to be given to the leading government party, the direction of the second

Gold, plastic, and lead   21

channel (RAI 2) to the second party in the government coalition, and the direction of the third channel to the opposition party. This type of power distribution is still valid today, even long after the demise of the three parties for which the system was originally created.

Carosello

As previously mentioned, much like the BBC, RAI's business model was based on a licence fee and a levy on the sales of TV sets, but it was also based on advertising revenues, which the BBC's "pure" public service model did not allow. The decision whether to allow television advertising was a highly debated and politically charged one since the beginning. Advertising had already been allowed in radio broadcasting, but the seductive power of moving images was a cause of increased concern for both ends of the Italian ideological spectrum. On the one end, the Catholic Church feared that "the insistent hammer blows of advertising pressure" (Ginsborg 1990: 248) would morally corrupt Italian households; on the other end, the Communist Party rejected television advertising as a by-product of American capitalism. The cultural and political debate regarding the fate of television advertising in Italy continued over the first years of RAI's service. Eventually, the Christian Democrat–led government settled on a compromise whereby advertising was allowed, but it had to be "boxed in" one single broadcast, as opposed to being scattered throughout the daily scheduling, as it was in the US television advertising model.[7] While the decision to allow advertising income was made very early on in the history of Italian public service broadcasters (PSBs), across Europe, PSBs made such shifts decades into their existence, mainly in the 1970s, though with important exceptions such as UK's BBC.

Carosello was the first advertising programme of Italian television, and the one that undoubtedly had the greatest influence on national society and culture ever since.[8] It was a 15-minute long segment that aired at 8:50 p.m. daily, which comprised a number of short comedy sketches (generally five, in animation and live action) that were paid for by advertisers. Plot structure and contents of each sketch had to adhere to rigorous regulations, set and overseen by a dedicated company, SACIS (*Società per Azioni Commerciale Iniziative Spettacolo*), under the broadcaster's control. *Carosello*'s opening tune was a 19th century *tarantella*, a tribute to Italian regional folk music, whereas the moving images showed theatre curtains opening onto statuette-like figures in Medieval costumes, a homage to traditional puppet theatre. The first episode of *Carosello* aired three years and one month after RAI's first official service, on February 3, 1957. It featured five sponsored sketches, the first of which being for the international oil company Shell. In

22 *Gold, plastic, and lead*

compliance with SACIS' regulation, the programme did not directly advertise Shell or its products, although its logo appeared in the backdrop of the scene. The sketch, titled "Shell's contribution to road security" (*Contributo Shell per la sicurezza del traffico*), was presented as a public service announcement, with the "acknowledgment of the Italian Automobile Club". In the sketch, popular sport journalist Giovanni Canestrini discussed advantages and disadvantages of left- versus right-hand traffic (only to leave the ultimate judgement to the viewers).

This very first *Carosello* sketch tells us at least two remarkable things about the culture that surrounded Italian advertising at that time, as well as its evolution to current times. Firstly, the Shell sketch embodied the quirky outcome of the political compromise that allowed advertising on Italian television in the first place. RAI needed extra funding from the private sector, so the Italian government allowed advertising. However, because of the ideological oppositions against it, the government also set rules whereby television advertising should not be explicitly presented as such, but instead disguised as entertainment, or even as a form of public announcement or educational message. The rationale behind these rules laid in the service contract which stated that advertising should be broadcast "in the most convenient forms so as not to prejudice the quality of the programmes" after (Ambrosino 2004: 293). Quite paradoxically, this goal of preserving the quality of programming, translated for RAI to the creation of a television format where advertising looked very much like regular entertainment. For example, *Carosello* very often featured serialised narratives, with recurring situations and catchphrases that were at all similar to sitcoms. Dorfles (1998) recalls that single episodes of *Carosello* were featured in RAI's listing magazine *Radiocorriere* as regular television programmes. Viewers were encouraged to not miss the upcoming *Carosello* episode for, say, Invernizzi cheese and its beloved character Susanna Tuttapanna, a happy-go-lucky, chubby cartoon girl; the new adventures of Gringo, the handsome cowboy of tinned meat Montana; or the duels between animated vulture Jo Condor, the villain, and the always triumphant good Giant that were featured in Nutella advertisements. The second remarkable trait that can be appreciated from the very first episode of *Carosello* is its resemblance to what is known today as *branded entertainment* (Lehu 2007). Branded entertainment, as a genre-specific form of branded content, consists of any entertainment product, most frequently in the video format, originally produced and creatively controlled by an advertiser. In this sense, the 2- to 3-minute video format, the predominance of entertainment over promotional messages, the framing in industry press as regular programming, and the fact that SACIS' regulation allowed each sketch to be aired a maximum of two times make *Carosello* more similar to contemporary forms of branded entertainment, rather than 30-second television commercials. Further proof

Gold, plastic, and lead 23

of such similarity is the fact that in 2005 the Italian coffee brand Lavazza decided to resume Carmencita, a Mexican-themed animated character of a highly popular *Carosello* first aired in 1965, this time as the protagonist of a transmedia branded storytelling experience, released across both traditional and new media.

With regard to the language and themes that *Carosello* portrayed, the SACIS' regulation imposed for every script to be pre-emptively controlled, amended and, if need be, eliminated, in the name of a prude ethical code. Censorship occurred for two main sets of reasons: public decency and political correctness. For instance, the terms *divorce* and *adultery*, and any situation somehow hinting to a family separation was forbidden to appear onscreen. Censorship applied to any word carrying even the slightest titillating potential, like *bra* or *underwear*, but also to any word referencing inelegant body functions, like *sweat* and *laxative*, even when the sketch was supposed to advertise a deodorant or a purgative drug. Political-based censorship aimed to avoid any situation that could potentially offend the sensitivity, on the one hand, of the Catholic, US-endorsed ruling party, and, on the other hand, of the politically defeated but still culturally influential, Soviet-backed Italian Communist party. The overzealousness of some of SACIS' officers has since become legendary, although sometimes the reasons for which a specific *Carosello* sketch was blocked have remained unfathomable. To this regard, famous Italian animation artist Bruno Bozzetto once recalled that he was forced to change the finale of a ludicrous sketch where a Cossack, well satiated with Perugina chocolates, goes on holiday to Hawaii (Canova 2004: 299). Was this considered harmful to the US (hence to the Christian democrat government) because it implied that USSR allowed total freedom of movement despite the Cold War? Or was it offensive to the USSR (hence the Italian Communist Party) because it showed a Russian character enjoying a capitalist lifestyle? No answer is available to such questions.

Carosello was on air for 20 years, with consistently high audience ratings. The reasons why RAI decided, in 1977, to discontinue the programme, despite its persistent success, are not fully known. Surely, as Dorfles (1998) suggested, advertisers were pushing for more spaces in television at lower prices, and this favoured the system of commercial breaks. Moreover, the growing diffusion of international consumer products pressured marketers to integrated, transnational advertising campaigns, whereas *Carosello*'s model was unique to Italy and hardly adaptable to foreign markets. Furthermore, the Parliamentary Commission, established with the 1975 reform law to oversee RAI's activities, could no longer tolerate that the most watched programme of Italian television was in fact an advertising programme. *Carosello* was especially popular among children to the point

24 *Gold, plastic, and lead*

of being defined as "a memorable collection of bedtime stories for the consumer age" (Annunziato and Fiumara 2015: 11).

As a format, *Carosello* was the single most influential programme in Italian television history, and the one which enabled television to earn an overpowering position over the other cultural industries. As Pitteri (2006) observed, the greatest loser in this battle for cultural relevance was Italian cinema. Ironically, Italian cinema shared with *Carosello* some of its best filmmakers and performers, as well as the technical facilities of Cinecittà Studios. To this regard, French auteur Jean-Luc Godard once made the provocative (but not entirely misplaced) statement that "the best Italian cinema is undoubtedly *Carosello*" (Mattelart 1991: 38).

1.4 Italy and the golden age of cinema

During the time span of the economic boom (mid-1950s–1960s), Italians discovered themselves for the first time as mass consumers. Increased spending did not only concern luxury goods, such as vehicles, furniture, and household appliances, but also cultural products and leisure activities. At that time, cinema was the single most popular form of commercial mass entertainment. In the 1950s, Italians were devoting around 70 per cent of their overall expenditure for leisure to cinemagoing, a figure in line with that of British and American consumers of the time (Treveri Gennari and Sedgwick 2015: 77). After steadily growing since the 1930s, annual sales of cinema tickets reached 819 million in 1955, which has thus remained the single most successful year for cinemagoing in Italy. That year, Italians attended film theatres an average of 17 times per person (Treveri Gennari and Sedgwick 2015). This was enabled by a capillary presence of theatres across the peninsula: commercial theatres, but also thousands of parish cinemas, often uncaptured by official statistics, which programmed first-, second-, and third-run films. In 1955, in Italy there was a cinema every 4565 inhabitants: for comparison's sake, 20 years later that ratio was grown to one cinema every 6254, and 40 years later to one every 15,013 (SIAE 1955, SIAE 1975). The peak in theatrical film consumption occurred in Italy at a time when attendances were already on a declining curve in the UK and in the US. Notably, the golden age of cinema occurred in Italy nearly a decade later than that of the Hollywood studios, as a result of the belated economic boom in Italy. However, the unprecedented, and ever unmatched, importance of cinema in 1950s Italy cannot be solely reduced to admissions and quantitative figures. Ethnohistorical studies of Italian cinema audiences have shown the great significance that cinemagoing had in those years as a socio-cultural practice.[9] Going to the cinema was a powerful individual experience, as well as a social ritual. For many Italians who were young

Gold, plastic, and lead 25

in the 1950s, going to the cinema was the only way to share an entertainment experience in close proximity with opposite-sex peers, away from the controlling gaze of parents and other authority figures. Moreover, as will be discussed in the next section, in a time of major social transformations, when television was yet to become a widespread household presence, cinema was a window onto unknown realities, starting from that close but all elusiveness of Italian cities and regions other than one's own.

Beside and beyond the prominence that cinema had from an economic and a socio-cultural perspective, the phrase "golden age" also refers to the high quality displayed by the Italian film production of that time. Films produced in Italy between the 1950s and 1970s showed levels of aesthetic and technical sophistication, as well as a drive for creative innovation that rarely found an equivalent in subsequent times. Bondanella and Pacchioni (2017) have traced this artistic peak back to the fact that during that period revered Italian directors, like Federico Fellini, Luchino Visconti, and Michelangelo Antonioni, produced their more mature works at the same time as a new wave of young, original auteurs, such as Ettore Scola, Bernardo Bertolucci, and Nanni Moretti, came on the scene.

How was this golden age of cinema spurred by policymaking and structural circumstances, in addition to individual talents? And how much of the aforementioned significance of cinema for Italian moviegoers was actually driven by national productions, as opposed to foreign, and notably American ones? In other words, how *Italian* was this golden age of cinema in Italy, and how has it affected the development of the country's film industry, as we all as the collective imagery surrounding Italy for years to come? The final sections of this chapter offer some answers to these complex questions.

Standing on shaky ground

The decades examined in this chapter are characterised, as we have seen, by dramatic transformations in the social, economic, and cultural fabric of the Italian nation. In the relatively brief time span of 20 years, Italy transitioned from being an underdeveloped, essentially rural society to becoming the world's fifth largest economy. Italy's new primary role in the global scenario also extended to the cultural sectors, and notably to cinema, which, as we have seen, enjoyed a golden age of popular as well as critical success. However, a closer look at the (actually rather scarce) studies[10] on the economic history of the Italian film industry reveals a far more nuanced reality. The post-war ideological battle that opposed the US to the Soviet Union, and their respective supporting parties in Italy, had significant repercussions on the reconstruction of the national film industry in the late 1940s and early 1950s. Notably, the foundations that were laid for the new, post-Fascist

26   *Gold, plastic, and lead*

national film industry to grow on were the rather shaky result of a compromise between the often-conflicting interests of domestic and foreign political and economic actors. Cinema was the terrain where the US strategy to combine industrial and cultural occupation in Italy unfolded more aggressively. However, cinema was also a sector where Italy had already gained sound experience and international achievements, and where Mussolini's autarchic policies were particularly impactful. Thus, unlike what would have soon happened in advertising and large-scale retailing, the Italian film industry associations succeeded in putting up a strong resistance against some of the government's concessions to US political pressure, which they perceived as detrimental to the interests of national cinema. Perhaps, the most spectacular example of such resistance was a widely attended public demonstration held on February 20, 1949, in Rome's central Piazza del Popolo. The demonstration was organised by national filmmakers, authors, and technicians united in a "Committee for the defense of Italian cinema", with the support of the National Association of Film Industries (ANICA). Among the points of contention was the government's decision to repeal a 15-year-old "dubbing tax", which allowed the Italian government to draw financial resources from foreign (especially American) films distributed in Italy and reallocate them to national productions. This decision, taken by the Christian Democrat government, was a concession to the Italian branches of Hollywood distribution majors, eager to take control of a strategic market in the Mediterranean region. Moreover, filmmakers and producers protested the lack of control over the implementation of minimum mandatory screen quota (80 days per year), which the law imposed for Italian-made films, but which exhibitors often evaded in favour of American titles (Treveri Gennari 2009). The government responded by issuing a law that neither really embraced nor fully rejected the demands coming from both national and US stakeholders. Law No. 958 of December 29, 1949, named the "Andreotti law" after the then government undersecretary in charge of entertainment, was the first comprehensive cinema reform law of the Italian Republic. It reintroduced mandatory payments for dubbing foreign pictures in Italian, not in the form of a tax, but rather as a "forced loan" (Treveri Gennari 2009: 50) that foreign film companies could subsequently claim back. The law preserved mandatory screen quota, but reassured exhibitors by stating that the minimum percentages would have been renegotiated on an annual basis. Moreover, and more important, the law, and its subsequent operative decrees, set up a broad system of public funding for national film productions (up to 60 per cent of the budget cost), but subordinated it to the pre-emptive control of the screenplay by the Cinema General Directorate. The Cinema General Directorate was a government-appointed office, first established under the Fascist regime, which centralised all the main activities

Gold, plastic, and lead 27

concerning the censorship, authorisation, funding, and promotion system of Italian film production.

The immediate effect of the Andreotti law was that state funds were distributed widely but thinly across national productions, and according to criteria that rewarded ideological acquiescence,[11] rather than artistic merit and economic sustainability. The result of this policy was a "production frenzy" (Corsi 2001: 51) that caused the number of new Italian releases to increase from 54 in 1948 to 164 in 1959 (SIAE). However, behind such quantitative growth was a "proliferation of botched production ventures" (Corsi 2001: 51), which often lived only for the time frame of a film but were nonetheless able to earn their founders easy state money.

Undersecretary Giulio Andreotti went on to perform important ministerial duties under the 22 Christian Democrat governments that came in succession since 1950. Then, in 1972, he became for the first time prime minister (a position he would hold for three different terms between 1972 and 1992).[12] Over those years, governments would have reformed national film policies multiple times, but the overall structure of distribution of state aids to Italian film productions, as it had been set by the 1949 Andreotti law, remained essentially unchanged until the new century. On the positive side, the Andreotti law allowed Italian cinema to survive, even to thrive during the golden age years and, most important, not to be completely swept away by Hollywood competition. On the negative side, the law also crystallised a system of "economic welfarism and political control" (Corsi 2001: 50–51), which brought the Italian film industry to grow fragmented and financially unstable. Financial and structural fragility are traits far removed from the US model, which Italian practitioners (both in the film and the advertising industries) still indicate as their reference point, as we will see further on in the book. The Andreotti law can be seen as the moment in time when some of the most fundamental (and still unresolved) contradictions within the Italian film industry first broke out—contradictions between openness to foreign models and protectionist measures; between state dependency and marketisation drives; between populist and elitist views of the audience; and, ultimately, between cinema as business and cinema as art.

Cinema as an advertising medium

During its golden years, cinema in Italy enjoyed extraordinary success in terms of the number of tickets sold, of its importance as a socio-cultural practice, and also of the quality of national productions. Its cross-demographic popularity made cinema the most powerful medium for all types of propaganda messages, at least until the widespread diffusion of television in Italian households. The very locations where film screenings took place, dark

28 *Gold, plastic, and lead*

and soundproof, helped the messages conveyed through that medium to resonate and stick with the audience. Indeed, during Fascism, every screening was preceded by a *cinegiornale*, a propaganda newsreel aimed to promote the regime's accomplishments. After the fall of the regime, these newsreels showed in overly positive light the difficult but heroic struggles of the government and of Italian enterprises to rebuild the country. The newsreel's political propaganda was followed by commercial advertisements, which exhibitors screened before the film and in between the first and second parts. Over the 1950s and into the 1960s, cinema accounted for a share between 5 and 6 per cent of the overall advertising media expenditures in Italy—much more than in the UK (1 to 1.5 per cent), the US (2.7 per cent) and second only to France (7 per cent) (Brigida, Baudi Di Vesme, and Francia 2004: 13).

The popularity of cinema in the 1950s was spurred as much by Italian policymakers' efforts to boost the national film industry, as by the US strategy to leverage motion pictures as means to establish their cultural hegemony in post-war Europe. In such context, advertising and consumer products proved instrumental for the purposes of both Italian and US stakeholders. On the one hand, films displayed consumer products and consumerist lifestyles that Italian audiences, eager to leave the deprivation of war behind and embrace the new economic boom, found particularly appealing. This was true of Hollywood pictures distributed in Italy, but also of a large part of domestic productions (with the important exception of Neorealist films). Indeed, during the golden age years:

> Even in populist dramas describing the situation of the poorest people, everything is perfectly decent. It is open to discussion whether this is some sort of indirect commercial advertisement, a way of promoting saleable goods by screening them, or whether films advertise themselves by providing viewers with the momentary personal pleasure of seeing beautiful objects and being introduced to the homes of the rich. Whatever the reasons, movies have long informed their spectators about up-to-date conventions or habits, they have promoted consumerism and introduced a sense of society as a source of pleasure.
>
> (Sorlin 1996: 4)

Advertisers soon became regular, if unofficial, economic contributors to Italian film productions through the practice of product placement. On the other hand, films became powerful windows for the promotion of *Made in Italy* products, and Italy itself became a brand to be advertised to international consumers, honouring the notion that "the culture that cinema advertises creates an image for the exporting country which redoubles export profits" (Sorlin 1996: 4).

Gold, plastic, and lead   29

This twofold process, which simultaneously promoted American culture to Italian moviegoers and Italy to American ones, is well epitomised by the case of 1953 award-winning, box office hit *Roman Holiday*, directed by William Wyler. *Roman Holiday* is the first American film to be almost entirely produced and post-produced outside the US. Paramount's decision to shoot the film on actual Roman locations was based on financial as well as aesthetic reasons. Financial reasons included the opportunity to access the federal tax shelter guaranteed to US film companies that operated at least 18 months abroad, as well as the opportunity to reinvest Paramount's capitals that were "frozen" in Italy as a result of protectionist measures (among which the aforementioned Andreotti law). Aesthetic reasons included the will to use Rome's stunning views to fascinate American audiences and create for them an experience of Italianness, which they could have recreated by travelling to the Eternal City (Shandley 2009).[13] The single most memorable sequence in *Roman Holiday* is certainly the one where Audrey Hepburn takes control of Gregory Peck's Vespa scooter and speeds off through the busy streets of the city centre, knocking down stands and disrupting the peace of outdoor café customers. This sequence only lasts a couple of minutes, but, together with the film's paratexts,[14] managed to transform the pressed steel scooter manufactured by Piaggio into a symbol of youth and freedom, as well as of a cheerful lifestyle that Americans too would have supposedly enjoyed when visiting Italy. Piaggio reportedly sold 100,000 Vespa units as a direct result of the scooter's appearance in Wyler's comedy hit.[15]

Interestingly, whilst *Roman Holiday* promoted Italy and a sugar-coated version of its post-war lifestyle to international audiences, it also introduced many Italians living in peripheral areas to their nation's capital city (Ercole, Treveri Gennari, and O'Rawe 2017). Indeed, before the household spread of television sets, Italians derived much of their sense of national identity from non-Italian, and notably, Hollywood films. This was the result of Italians' fascination with American culture and their appetite for new, affluent sociocultural models, but it also derived from the large market share of US films that were screened in Italian theatres. In 1949, US productions accounted for 73 per cent of the Italian market share, against 17.3 per cent of national productions (Corsi 2001: 34). Since 1950, the market shares of US versus Italian films progressively evened as a result of state policies boosting domestic production. Market shares of national films steadily grew throughout the decade, and in 1960 they overtook for the first time those of US films (50.6 versus 35.6 per cent). The taste for national productions that Italian audiences clearly displayed through the 1960s and until the mid-1970s can be seen as part of a Europe-wide trend. The popularity of European cinema of the time was, from an artistic perspective, linked to the works of

30 *Gold, plastic, and lead*

great coeval auteurs, such as Federico Fellini, Michelangelo Antonioni, and Luchino Visconti in Italy; François Truffaut and Jean-Luc Godard in France; and Ingmar Bergman in Sweden. In Italy, those years also saw the successful renewal of popular film genres such as the Italian-style comedy (*commedia all'italiana*), the spaghetti western, and the romantic comedy. From a production perspective, Italian and European producers managed to confront Hollywood competition by frequently turning to international co-productions, which not only allowed for the use of bigger budgets and international talents, but also guaranteed cross-national distribution.

The film that best represents this fortunate period for Italian, and more broadly European, cinema is arguably *La Dolce Vita* (1960). Federico Fellini's box office hit *La Dolce Vita* was an Italian-French co-production, starring an international cast that included Marcello Mastroianni, Anita Ekberg, and Anouk Aimée. Besides being an all-time masterpiece of Italian cinema, *La Dolce Vita* bears two characteristics that make it particularly relevant to the issues approached by this book. Firstly, the film offers an image of Italy and Italianness, which significantly influenced not only subsequent films, both national and international, but also advertising, television series, and the whole visual imagery related to the country. Secondly, *La Dolce Vita* can be considered as one of the first, and certainly most successful, cases of transmedia storytelling in the history of Italian cinema. To this regard, Italian film critic Tullio Kezich defined *La Dolce Vita* as a "tabloid-film" (*film-rotocalco*) (Costa 2010) because of the close relation connecting it to the tabloid magazines of the time. The dialogical relationship between film and magazines started well before the shooting began, in March 1959, at the Cinecittà studios. The very sequence where Anita Ekberg plunges in the Trevi fountain had a real-life antecedent in 1958, which Italian tabloids widely reported. The film enjoyed continuous press coverage throughout production and after its much-debated theatrical release. Politicians and intellectuals divided between those who despised the film for painting a decadent picture of Italian society and those who praised it for shedding light onto the dark side of the "Hollywood on the Tiber", as the city was known since William Wyler's *Roman Holiday*. What is most interesting to remark, though, is that much of these sensationalistic reports came from illustrated magazines, such as *L'Europeo* and *Oggi*, which were owned by Italian publisher Angelo Rizzoli, who also controlled Cineriz, the film company that produced and distributed *La Dolce Vita*. Thus, film and tabloids mutually fed and advertised each other, with an ingenious strategy of synergistic activities that, whilst common in modern days, was unprecedented at that time. Just like in modern-day transmedia campaigns, *La Dolce Vita* also contributed to promote the fashion styles and consumable items portrayed in the film. For example, the turtleneck jumper worn by Pierone (Giò

Stajano), one of the colourful characters that populated the bars and parties in the film, became so popular as to be renamed *dolcevita*; the term has since been officially introduced in Italian vocabularies to define that type of garment. Moreover, in the scene where protagonist Marcello takes his father to a nightclub in via Veneto, he is seen and heard ordering a Black & White whisky. The film also made iconic the sunglasses that Marcello Mastroianni's character wore throughout the film, even at night time, and that were manufactured by Italian brand Persol. Fifty-five years later, Persol celebrated the anniversary with a branded entertainment initiative that centred around a *La Dolce Vita*-inspired short film, directed by German auteur Wim Wenders: "Vai, paparazzo!" (2015). This type of branded insertions, which we now call product placement, was not uncommon at that time, although the practice only became widespread in Italian cinema since the 1970s. Interestingly, advertising *in films* increased at the same time as advertising *in cinemas* was declining: from 5–6 per cent in 1960 to 4.4 per cent in 1975, mostly as result of the decrease in theatrical attendance (819 million tickets sold in 1955, 663 million in 1965, and 514 million in 1975) (Corsi 2003: 833).

Product placement in Italian cinema would not become a proper business until its legalisation in 2004. However, as early as the 1960s, when *La Dolce Vita* came out, it was not uncommon for Italian filmmakers to "adjust" camera movements and editing to give exposure to a certain product or brand. It was the so-called *pubblicità occulta* (surreptitious advertising), and it was illegal not because specific laws prevented it,[16] but rather because such advertising was paid by under the table money. The advertiser directly paid the director, sometimes the producer, and, if need be, the acting star involved in the placement scene. From the filmmakers' perspective, this was a quick and relatively harmless way to make extra money out of a film whose commercial performance was ever more uncertain. From the advertisers' perspective, it was the only screen media advertising alternative available to the costlier and heavily restricted *Carosello*. Moreover, for tobacco and alcohol manufacturers, for which television advertising was, respectively, banned and heavily constrained, there simply was no alternative. As a result, Italian cinemagoers became accustomed to the numerous, and yet somewhat unexplainable, close-ups of cigarette packages and branded ashtrays, or to the longer-than-usual shots devoted to whisky bottles on a bar counter, or to the giant outdoor billboard of a liqueur brand. Among the most frequently placed companies were Marlboro and Muratti for cigarettes; and Martini, Cynar, and Fernet Branca for alcohol drinks (Corti 2004). However, the practice also concerned product categories that were not prevented from advertising in other media: mineral water Pejo and liquid soap Vidal were particularly recurrent. This practice was especially

32   *Gold, plastic, and lead*

widespread in the 1970s to the point of becoming an object of satire by Italian auteur Nanni Moretti in his second feature film *Ecce Bombo* (1978). While talking to an actress friend, Michele (played by Moretti himself) asks her:

> Has it ever occurred to you to play in a film where a cigarette brand is promoted? The actor and the director share the money, and the actor says [holding a cigarette pack towards her] "Would you like a cigarette?". Manfredi, he is the cheekiest one, says [holding the cigarette pack so as to face the camera]: "Would you like a cigarette?"

Moretti's reference here is to actor Nino Manfredi, who starred in many popular, and product placement-filled, comedies during the 1970s.

Notes

1 Italy's territorial borders have continued to evolve well into the 20th century, with the most significant changes being the annexation of the current regions of Trentino Alto Adige and Friuli Venezia Giulia following World War I, which is in fact also known as Italy's Fourth War of Independence. For a succinct but comprehensive analysis of the *Risorgimento* and its continuous resonance in the political and cultural history of modern Italy, see Riall (1994).
2 In this context, the preferred term is *Italianness* over that of *Italianicity*, employed, in particular, by Roland Barthes (1977); the latter is closely connected to the theoretical and methodological framework of semiotic studies, whereas the former is more commonly used in media and cultural studies.
3 Films of the 1960s and 1970s have often portrayed the material and psychological struggles suffered by Italians migrating during the years of the economic miracle. Notably, Luchino Visconti's *Rocco and His Brothers* (1960) tells the dramatic story of a family moving from the Southern region of Basilicata to a basement flat in the periphery of Milan, whereas Ermanno Olmi's *Il Posto* ("The position") follows a young man in his quest for a secure office job from a village in Lombardy to the big city.
4 For a comprehensive examination of the diplomatic effort of the US to advertise the American lifestyle in post-war Italy, see Tobia (2008).
5 For an analysis of how Italian filmmakers have represented the Years of Lead, see O'Leary (2010).
6 In Spain, Televisión Española began regular transmissions in 1956, one year earlier than Rádio e Televisão de Portugal. In the UK, BBC launched regular service in 1936; in France, Radio-PTT Vision started broadcasting in 1935; and in Germany, Deutscher Fernseh Rundfunk began regular transmissions in 1935 (Brevini 2013).
7 Until the mid-1950s, advertising money was poured into US television mostly in the form of single-sponsorship programming (Boddy 1990), which gave advertisers direct control over the content (and sometimes even the name) of the programmes, e.g. *The Philco Television Playhouse* (NBC, 1948–1955), *Texaco Star Theatre* (NBC, 1948–1956), and *Camel News Caravan* (NBC,

Gold, plastic, and lead   33

1949–1956). Single-sponsorship programming was replaced by spot advertising following the infamous *The $64,000 Question* quiz show scandal, which revealed how advertisers had been manipulating quiz competitions to favour brand-friendly contestants. Moreover, spot advertising allowed broadcasters to capitalise on high-rating shows by selling the airtime slots within those shows to multiple buyers.

8 The exact origin of the name *Carosello* is unclear, but it alludes to childhood: either a ball game popular during the Spanish domination (15th–16th centuries) or the Neapolitan dialect word for children's moneyboxes, *carusielli* (Dorfles 1998: 16).

9 To this regard, in addition to the already cited works of Forgacs and Gundle (2007) and Treveri Gennari and Sedgwick (2015), see also Ercole, Treveri Gennari, and O'Rawe (2017); Treveri Gennari, O'Rawe, and Hipkins (2011); and, in Italian, Fanchi and Mosconi (2002).

10 English-written literature specifically devoted to the economic dimension of Italian film history is scarce. Exceptions are to be found in Christopher Wagstaff's (1995) and, more recently, in Marina Nicoli's books (2011, 2017). For Italian-language readers, Barbara Corsi's works (2001, 2012) on the history of Italian film production and film producers are essential readings.

11 For example, the animosity of the Christian Democrat government towards the social and political criticism expressed by Neorealist films is well known. Government undersecretary Giulio Andreotti reportedly criticised Vittorio De Sica's drama *Umberto D.* (1952), which tells the story of a poor elderly man who commits suicide because he is no longer able to afford his rented room with minimum pension, by commenting: "Dirty laundry shall not be washed in public" ("*I panni sporchi si lavano in famiglia*").

12 Giulio Andreotti's long political career, which marked, for better or for worse, many of the main events in 20th century Italian history, found representation in Paolo Sorrentino's film *Il Divo* (2008).

13 In recent years, the practice of using films and other screen contents to promote tourism in selected places has been defined *location* or *destination placement*, and it is closely connected to the activities of film commissions around the world. For an in-depth analysis of film-induced tourism, see Beeton (2005), in English, and Cucco and Richeri (2013), in Italian.

14 Gregory Peck and Audrey Hepburn are portrayed on the Vespa scooter in many versions of the original poster, as well as in the movie's original trailer made for US distribution.

15 Vespa's notoriety and its status as a symbol of Italian style were later reinforced through several appearances in popular films set in Italy and abroad, e.g. *To Catch a Thief* (dir. Hitchcock, 1955), *Poveri ma belli* (UK title *A Girl in Bikini*; dir. Risi, 1957), *La Dolce Vita* (dir. Fellini, 1960), *Jessica* (dir. Negulesco, 1962), *Alfie* (dir. Gilbert, 1966), *American Graffiti* (dir. Luca, 1973), *Quadrophenia* (dir. Roddam, 1979), and, more recently, in *Caro Diario* (dir. Moretti, 1993), *The Talented Mr. Ripley* (dir. Minghella, 1999), and *Zoolander 2* (dir. Stiller, 2016).

16 The first legal ban of surreptitious advertising came in 1990 as a result of the transposition of the European Union directive "Television Without Frontiers".

2 The normalisation of anomaly

Italy between the 1980s
and the 2000s

2.1 Media, advertising, and politics: the years of convergence

The events presented in this chapter encompass 30 years of Italy's recent history, from the beginning of the 1980s to the end of the 2000s, which had powerful, and in many ways still ongoing, effects on the political, social, and cultural state of the country. These three decades were marked by radical transformations at all levels of Italy's public life, as well as by profound changes in how individuals perceived and engaged themselves in relation to public life. These were also years during which dramatic events in domestic politics caused the image of Italy on the international stage to change. Interestingly, during this time, Italian filmmakers mostly chose not to comment on such events directly (apart for few exceptions), or they did it marginally, and instead preferred to focus on more private, inward-looking stories. This trend in cinematic representation can be actually seen as part of a broader socio-cultural trend that invested Italian society at the turn of the 1980s, which sociologists and commentators of the time called *riflusso* ("backlash"; Arvidsson 2003: 105). The term *riflusso*, which literally describes the receding flow of a wave from the shore towards the sea, came to metaphorically identify a retreat to the private sphere after the tumultuous and publicly engaged social life of the previous decade. As we shall see shortly, advertising and consumer culture played a major role in shaping the newly individualised and, to a large extent, politically disengaged Italian society in the 1980s. The decade that was about to begin was also the one when consumer brands retained an unprecedented importance for conveying meanings of social affiliation.

Italians' renewed consumerism at the turn of the 1980s was not only the result of an ideological, or better post-ideological attitude, but it also derived from changes in the economic situation of the country. The 1981 population census (ISTAT 1981) showed for the first time that Italians

The normalisation of anomaly 35

employed in the service sector exceeded those in industrial production and agriculture. There were persistent disparities across the regions, notably between the more advanced North and the South. However, these data meant, as Forgacs (2000) has observed, that Italy had made the transition from being a pre-industrial to a post-industrial society in a time span of less than two generations. Italy's strong economic growth, which began in the mid-1950s, continued without interruption (except for the relatively brief period of austerity following the international oil crisis of 1973) until the end of the 1980s. At the turn of the 1990s, though, things changed and a series of financial as well as political crises hit the country, namely a strong devaluation of the Italian currency and the nationwide corruption scandal *Tangentopoli* ("Bribesgate"). As a result of the economic downturn of the early 1990s, and spurred by the boom of hard discount stores, Italian consumers moved away from consumer brands, which had driven purchase decisions in the previous decade, and turned to unbranded, cheaper products. As we shall see in the next section, advertising played a key role in restoring consumers' faith in brands, by adapting communications to the much less euphoric climate of 1990s' Italy.

With regard to the evolution of the media landscape, this chapter looks at a time span of major technological changes, which also entailed a reconfiguration of people's understanding of media from a socio-cultural standpoint. During the 30 years between the beginning of the 1980s and the end of the 2000s, Italian television moved from having three nationwide channels, broadcast through analogue terrestrial technology by a public service monopolist, to over a hundred channels, transmitted by public and private, Italian and international operators across analogue and digital, terrestrial, cable, and satellite technologies. From a political-economic perspective, the Italian television market went through transformations that were both country-specific and worldwide. As to the former, this period saw the demise of RAI's public "monopoly cycle" and the emergence, and then partial overcoming, of a public–private "duopoly cycle" between RAI and Berlusconi's Fininvest/Mediaset (Richeri 2009). As to the latter, the 2000s also saw the boom of an era of "media fragmentation" (Napoli 2011) that has been characterising the global scenario ever since. During these years, the cinematic medium has been undergoing a similar process of decentralisation, having moved beyond the collective domain of film theatres, into further, mostly private places of consumption, which often entailed smaller screens: free-to-air television, video home system (VHS), video on demand (VOD), and digital video recorders (DVRs) have progressively become privileged instruments for film consumption. At the same time, during the 1990s, film theatres across Italy moved from a single to a multi-screen model (the multiplex). Digital technology allowed for greater image and sound quality, and

36 *The normalisation of anomaly*

led to a resurgence of three-dimensional (3D) films, all of which boosted theatrical attendance and increased box office results.

Scholars and commentators around the world have devoted a sheer amount of work to describe and critically analyse the complex transformative phenomena that concerned all aspects of media production, distribution, and consumption between the 1980s and 2000s. The single most successful term that came to designate the processes and outcome of such transformations is that of *convergence* (Jenkins 2006). Convergence occurs at a technological level, as seen in the emergence of devices, such as smartphones, that perform tasks and functions that were previously prerogative of distinct products. It occurs at an industrial level, with the merging of previously separated sectors and companies, via processes of vertical and horizontal integration (Disney's acquisition of Pixar being a prominent example of the latter). Convergence also occurs at a cultural level, as audiences are both consumers and creators of media content, as the practice of fan fiction writing well exemplifies (see Hardy 2013, for a concise and Lugmayr and Dal Zotto 2016, for an extensive review of the different perspectives on convergence in the media sector). Advertising and marketing are integral components of this convergence culture, not only because advertisers provide essential financial resources to media producers, but also because the messages advertisers convey often contribute to the same aesthetic and symbolic universe that media producers create.

In the Italian case, the convergence between cinema, television, and advertising is both direct and indirect, and it operates at the economic as well as the aesthetic level. From an economic perspective, advertisers' influence on Italian filmmaking is mediated by the main national broadcasters, which control a large part of the film production and distribution market. RAI and Mediaset's financial contribution accounts for an estimated 40–45 per cent of Italian films' production budgets (MiBACT 2016; Barra and Scaglioni 2017), whereas in the distribution market, their subsidiaries 01 Distribution and Medusa Film control market shares of, respectively, 8.4 per cent and 14.9 per cent (the latter being the second top distributor, after Warner Bros.) (AGCM 2017). However, advertisers' influence on Italian cinema also exerts directly (and increasingly so, as we shall see), thanks to specific funding measures that reward, through significant tax incentives, consumer companies that invest in national film production. From an aesthetic perspective, a vast portion of Italian film production, and notably the films at the top positions in the box office rankings, closely resembles television advertising. On the one hand, this is the result of the growing use of (sometimes ridiculously prominent) product placement, as we shall in Chapter 3. On the other hand, though, this also derives from an aesthetic of "prettiness" (Galt 2013), which characterises many Italian films and

The normalisation of anomaly   37

makes them visually akin to television advertisements. In a 2003 magazine article, film critic Marco Giusti wrote, with regard to contemporary Italian filmmakers:

> They don't create their images on the basis of a familiarity with the works of Masaccio or Giotto. They work using commercials from Telecom or for the Banca di Roma as their models. (…) adverts which they themselves have shot. They think that modern montage, with continuous jumps cuts, is the answer to every problem in terms of expression. Or that a trendy director of photography can provide everything that a film needs as regards rhythm, particularly comedies. Or that a song from the Sixties by Patti Pravo or Nada can make a scene poetic. There isn't a single Italian director who hasn't slipped one of these songs in.
>
> (Giusti 2003, quoted in Hope 2005: 19–20)

Giusti's statement highlights what may be considered the biggest criticism of the films made in Italy during the last 20 to 30 years: the reliance on a televisual, and more precisely an advertising-like, kind of aesthetic. Such trend applies, albeit with some differences, to films made mostly for a domestic audience, as well as to Italian films with international ambitions. In the upcoming pages, we will dig into the policy, economic, and sociocultural factors that contributed to bringing contemporary Italian cinema close to a branded form of audio-visual entertainment.

2.2 Politics as marketing, marketing politics

Italy, between the 1950s and 1970s, experienced major economic and social changes, but it also enjoyed a long period of political stability. The Christian Democracy Party had been leading Italian governments uninterruptedly from the immediate post-war up to the end of the 1970s. Such continuity was politically and financially backed by American governments, which considered Italy as a fundamental outpost in the Cold War against the Soviet Union. On the domestic front, the Christian Democrat governments, whilst welcoming the US's alliance to hold back the political advance of the Italian Communist Party, also put in place protectionist measures to avoid a complete economic subordination to the powerful ally. Film policies were a clear example of this twofold strategy, which allowed the Christian Democracy to get the national film industry back on its feet, but in the framework of governmental censorship. The political marginalisation of the Communist Party continued to be a paramount goal of Italian governments well after the 1970s. However, as we shall see in the next section, Italy's

38   *The normalisation of anomaly*

political climate was changing. At the turn of the 1980s and again in the 1990s, major corruption scandals hit Italian politics, which eventually led to the demise of all the former governing parties. What resulted was a national political earthquake that, coupled with the international crisis of traditional political ideologies that followed the fall of the Berlin Wall, led to the rise of new political forces: first and foremost Silvio Berlusconi's Forza Italia. The defining trait of Italy's new political class was a strong reliance on its leaders' persona against the backdrop of a relatively weakly structured party system. A trend towards personalisation of politics was not unique to Italy—to this regard, Mancini (2011) also mentions the case of France's former President Nicolas Sarkozy—but Berlusconi's case is certainly paradigmatic. Long-established ideologies and political beliefs gave way to a more fragmented and highly individualistic set of values. In such a context, which mostly rewarded personal charisma and narratives of self-made manhood, consumerism subsumed political participation, or more precisely, consumerism became a kind of political value. Advertising, cinema, and television are the fields where such intertwining of politics and consumerism played out publicly and most effectively, as we shall see in further detail over the following sections.

The Italian videocracy

As previously mentioned, the 1980s opened tragically with the Bologna massacre. The decade went on to a fast-paced succession of two Christian Democrat-led governments. The latter of them fell in the spring of 1981 because of some of its ministries' involvement in the so-called P2 scandal. P2, standing for "Propaganda 2", was a clandestine, ultraright-wing Masonic lodge believed to be involved in high-profile terrorist acts—including the Bologna massacre—and to be ultimately attempting a coup plot. The political and juridical turmoil that ensued led to the end of the Christian Democratic governments and to the creation of a five-party coalition (known as *pentapartito*) that ruled the country throughout the 1980s. The coalition government headed by Socialist Party secretary Bettino Craxi between 1983 and 1987 was particularly impactful on the Italian media system, as it issued a series of decrees that allowed Berlusconi's then nascent television empire to flourish, despite multiple adverse juridical acts.

A decade after the P2 scandal, another major judicial investigation broke out causing the disruption and eventual dismissal of virtually Italy's entire political class: a nationwide corruption scandal known as *Tangentopoli* (Bribesgate). A Milan-based pool of magistrates uncovered a well-established system of corruption between entrepreneurs and politicians for the adjudication of public procurement contracts. Former Prime Minister

The normalisation of anomaly   39

Bettino Craxi was also involved in the scandal, along with nearly half of the then Italian MPs. The MPs' decision to save Craxi from arrest, which had resulted not so much from corporative solidarity as from fear of his potential revelations, caused violent outrage in the Italian public opinion. The day after the Parliament's vote, hundreds of people gathered outside Craxi's hotel in Rome and, as he left the building to get in a car, started throwing coins and chanting slurs at him. This episode was captured on camera and broadcast by national media over and over again, just like any other moment of the whole investigation that was relentlessly mediatised, sometimes with tragic consequences.[1] Craxi eventually fled the country and spent the rest of his life in Tunisia. The Bribesgate scandal swept away the parties that had been running the country for the previous 45 years. In 1994, both the Christian Democracy and the Socialist Party, the parties most implicated in the scandal, effectively dissolved overnight. The head of state appointed for the first time a non-member of the Parliament as prime minister. It was the end of Italy's so-called First Republic.

At the same time as traditional parties were crumbling, and eventually disappeared from the public sphere, a new political entity was about to appear onto the scene. On January 26, 1994, the evening news programmes of all the national television channels broadcast a nine-minute pre-registered video message featuring media mogul Silvio Berlusconi sitting at the desk of his home office. In this message, Berlusconi publicly announced his decision to "enter the field"[2] and running in the upcoming general elections with his newly funded political party: Forza Italia.[3] In his (already presidential in tone) address to the nation, Berlusconi presented himself as a champion of individual freedom and economic liberalism, who wanted to prevent "the Communists" and the old political class from gaining power. In two months, Berlusconi's popular consensus grew massively, and at the March 1994 elections, where it ran in alliance with the separatist party of Northern League and the neo-fascists of National Alliance, Forza Italia became the most voted single party.

With regard to the issues at stake in this book, two aspects of Berlusconi's political beginnings are particularly relevant: firstly, the paramount role that Publitalia, the advertising branch of Berlusconi's media group, played in the creation of his political party, and secondly, the style of his communication, which relied in unprecedented ways on personalisation, and ultimately produced a "mediatization of the political sphere" (Mazzoleni 1995: 307). As to the former aspect, Berlusconi drew on Publitalia's human and organisational resources to create and institutionalise his political base. Unlike traditional parties, Forza Italia did not originate from grassroots participation, but from a top-down initiative. This meant that the party did not have a capillary presence, in the form of local branches, across the country. To

40 *The normalisation of anomaly*

solve this structural flaw, Berlusconi commissioned Marcello Dell'Utri, then president of Publitalia, to create a network of "Forza Italia clubs", which had to build his consensus nationwide. The first Forza Italia clubs were established by Publitalia's young and efficient team of salesmen, who were used to travelling across the country to seek new advertisers for Berlusconi's television channels. In fact, the clubs operated according to a commercial franchise model: each founder received a "kit", which was essentially a Forza Italia merchandise pack that he or she could use to brand the new club. Forza Italia's political identity was effectively built according to the rules of corporate marketing. Indeed, the party's leaders were chosen among Publitalia's top management executives.

As to the second point of relevance, Berlusconi's political ascent caused, from the very beginning, serious concerns for the state of democracy and pluralism in Italy. When he first "entered the field", Berlusconi had been controlling the private side of the duopoly that constituted the Italian television market for a decade. Given the political carveout characterising RAI's governance (*lottizzazione*), as soon as he became prime minister, Berlusconi was virtually in control of the entire television market in Italy. Such a blatant conflict of interests was an abnormal singularity in Western democracies. Italian and international commentators of the time raised the question of whether, given such conditions, Italy was becoming a "videocracy" (Mazzoleni 1995) or a "telecracy" (Sznajder 1995), a nation whose political system had been appropriated by the television medium. In hindsight, the influence of Berlusconi's media was not so much exerted as a form of direct political propaganda, which left-wing newspapers, intellectuals, and part of the public service broadcaster managed to counterbalance. Rather, the videocracy that Berlusconi's media succeeded in establishing was actually a new type of society. As political philosopher Norberto Bobbio bitterly wrote in the aftermath of Berlusconi's first electoral victory:

> The society that has been created by television is naturally a society of the right. (...) It is not Berlusconi who won, it is the society that his mass media organizations have created that won. This is the society that enjoys looking at stupid families sitting around a table celebrating this or that product.
>
> (Bobbio 1994, quoted in Mancini 2011: 3)

So, what were the main features of the Italian society that Silvio Berlusconi was able to leverage, and at the same time contributed to create, and that sanctioned the success of his media enterprise as well as of his political party? How was their relation to politics and entertainment media? And

The normalisation of anomaly 41

how has such society evolved into the 2000s? The next section addresses such questions.

Italy to drink

At the turn of the 1970s, Italian society experienced a period of general retreat from public engagement into more private, individualistic ways of life (Arvidsson 2003). In this sense, Italy was no exception, as other Western countries were experiencing similar trends, which American political scientist Lance Bennett summarised in the notion of "lifestyle politics":

> The psychological energy (cathexis) people once devoted to the grand political projects of economic integration and nation-building in industrial democracies is now increasingly directed toward personal projects of managing and expressing complex identities in a fragmenting society.
>
> (Bennett 1998: 755)

In early 1980s Italy, such a trend was not so much a by-product of the implementation of the governmental neoliberalist policies, as it was a reaction to the traumatic Years of Lead, and the terrorist acts and political divisions that had characterised them.

From an economic perspective, the turn of the 1980s saw an upturn in Italy's GDP (+3 to +4 per cent annually between 1983 and 1987), which was defined a "mini-boom", or a "second economic miracle", after the main one of the late 1950s (Arvidsson 2003: 130–131). Consistently with the new psycho-sociological climate of the country, Italians devoted much of their increased affluence to private consumption. In a period of general political disengagement, Italians, and notably youths, turned to consumption as a means to construct and perform their identities. The 1980s were a decade when consumer culture earned unprecedented importance in Italy and, unsurprisingly, this coincided with advertisers starting to engage with new branding techniques and lifestyle marketing. If, between the 1950s and 1960s, the city of Rome had been the symbolic centre of a certain lifestyle—decadent, hedonistic, and "sweet" (*La dolce vita* means "The sweet life")—then in the 1980s Milan became the image of a different type of society. This society was "positive, optimistic, efficient", it woke up early in the morning with a smile on the face, took a taxi to work, and had a lifestyle "to be dreamt, to be enjoyed, to be drunk" (Amaro Ramazzotti 1985). At least, such were the claims of a popular television advertisement for a liqueur manufactured by Milan-based brand Amaro Ramazzotti, whose tagline *Milano da bere* ("Milan to drink") came to define the whole 1980s

42 *The normalisation of anomaly*

decade.[4] The swinging lifestyle portrayed in Amaro Ramazzotti's and in other advertising campaigns of the 1980s also found representation in the programming of the then newly established commercial television, which was characterised by light entertainment, in explicit contrast to the more uptight programming of the public service broadcaster. The airtime of early commercial television was mostly devoted to advertisements and infomercials, variety shows with sexy dancers and showgirls, and cheap serial programmes bought from abroad, such as US-made soap operas and sitcoms, Latin American *telenovelas*, and Japanese cartoons. Moreover, in the mid-1980s, commercial televisions started picking up some of the contents and styles of commercial radios, either by broadcasting 24-hour music channels (such as Videomusic, the Italian equivalent and forerunner of US channel MTV, which came in 1997) or individual programmes devoted to pop music videos and charts, the most popular being *DeeJay Television*, which exclusively programmed US and British bands and was broadcast by Berlusconi's channels. Like in other Western countries, 1980s pop music and its televised music videos, which strongly emphasised visual elements, proved powerful media for the dissemination of consumer culture. In Italy, though, such emphasis on aesthetics engendered a peculiar youth subculture, unsurprisingly originating in Milan, whose members identified themselves on the basis of which pop music and which commercial brands they consumed. This subculture was named *Paninari* ("sandwichers"), because they used to gather at the then newly opened Italian fast food restaurant Burghy, a now defunct equivalent to McDonald's. *Paninari* listened to synth pop and new romantic bands such as Duran Duran and Spandau Ballet,[5] loved Hollywood blockbuster movies like *Top Gun* (dir. Tony Scott, 1986), and, most important, purchased very specific (and expensive) clothing brands, both Italian and international: Timberland boots, Moncler down jackets, Levi's jeans, Invicta rucksacks, and Naj-Oleari satchels, to name a few. As critical sociologist Adam Arvidsson has observed:

> Although, in many respects, the heirs of the Neo-Fascist subculture of the 1970s, politics proper had little or no relevance for the *paninari*. Rather, their main interests were the timeless concern of the careless: fun, parties, petty romances and, above all, style, surrounding themselves with the 'right' mix of objects.
>
> (Arvidsson 2003: 126)

Similar observations can be made about the sociological profiles of the characters represented in a series of Italian films that began their long and lucky box office history in the same period: the *cinepanettoni*. The journalistic term *cinepanettoni*, coined with pejorative intent in the early 2000s, came

The normalisation of anomaly   43

to retrospectively identify a series of comic films released annually around Christmas time (*panettone* is the typical Italian Christmas pudding). The first title of the series, *Vacanze di Natale* ("Christmas holidays", dir. Carlo Vanzina) was released in 1983. The cinepanettoni were characterised by a series of production, as well as narrative, recurring traits: they were made by the same company (Filmauro, owned by the De Laurentiis family); they starred popular comedians Christian De Sica and Massimo Boldi; they used fancy touristic destinations as film locations; their soundtracks included the latest pop hits; and their comedy was often crass, based on bad language, scatological jokes, and female nudity. The whole universe of cinepanettoni revolved around consumption: the term itself suggests "that the films are a matter of mere consumption, a kind of cultural over-indulgence when the spectator is already full, akin to the slice of *panettone* ingested after a substantial Christmas meal" (O'Leary 2011: 432). Moreover, their plots and comedy twists were often based on the attempts of a goodhearted but penniless young man to fit in an affluent and materialistic social environment in order to win the beautiful girl over. The paninari youth subculture, with its consumerist values and general neglect for social and political engagement, was the perfect target audience of this type of comedies.

The cinepanettoni series continued through the 1990s and 2000s, but Italians' relationship to consumer brands progressively changed. After the consumerist feast of the 1980s, encouraged by the economic "mini-boom", the 1990s started off with a dramatic decline in the national economy. In 1993, the year of the *Mani Pulite* scandal, the Italian GDP lost a staggering 20 per cent and the purchasing power of the Italian lira was on a downturn spiral: if, in 1983, 10,000 Italian liras had roughly the same purchase power as 15 euros of today (13.5 GBP), in 1993 that figure had decreased to 8 euros (7 GBP) (historical exchange rates by the Italian National Institute of Statistics). Private consumption decreased accordingly, and consumer brands were particularly affected. This was partly due to Italian consumers' increased maturity and selectiveness, but it was also the result of the arrival in Italy of hard-discount distribution. Already successful in France and Germany, hard-discount retailers offered unbranded products at very reduced rates. Among the inflation-struck Italian society of the mid-1990s, hard-discount enjoyed immediate success. The reactions of Italian brands to this situation consisted, in some cases, in a reduction of prices, but primarily in the implementation of new types of advertising communications.

Two main communication models can be discerned in the advertising campaigns of Italian brands in the 1990s. On the one hand, brands started to link their communications to important social and political issues. The most prominent example of this trend was the provocative print advertising campaigns created for Benetton clothing brand by Italian photographer

44 *The normalisation of anomaly*

Oliviero Toscani, which recycled documentary pictures representing issues such as racism, migration, and the HIV epidemic (the "catastrophe ad series"; Falk 1997: 76). The campaigns were effective in raising Benetton brand awareness worldwide, but they also drew strong criticism for allegedly commodifying tragic events and phenomena (Giroux 1994). On the other hand, advertisers associated brands to stronger brand values, such as high-quality products, research and development, and trustworthiness. From a creative perspective, long-established brands did so by resuming the tradition of *Carosello*. The most successful advertisements of the 1990s were actually created by the same Italian agency, Armando Testa, that had previously been responsible for the creation of some of the most memorable *Carosello* programmes. These ads thus adopted the serialised format, with characters and comical situations recurring from one instalment to the next. These advertising campaigns shared another creative feature that continued throughout the 1990s and 2000s: a strong reliance on popular film and television personalities, both in front and behind the camera. For example, the star of cinepanettoni Christian De Sica played an underprepared grocer in a series of spots for Parmacotto ham; Academy award winner Gabriele Salvatores (Mediterraneo, 1991) directed a popular campaign for the coffee brand Lavazza, and television comedian Massimo Lopez starred in the advertisements for Italian telecommunication service Sip, under the direction of filmmaker Alessandro D'Alatri. Italy's widespread use of television and film personalities, whilst successful in the domestic market, constituted a creative setback by comparison with international trends in advertising creativity of the time. It is interesting to note that some of the "communication shortcuts" that Italian creatives used in popular advertising campaigns of 1990s and 2000s were also used by Italian filmmakers of the time, and notably: "testimonials from the world of entertainment, catchy pop songs, female as well as male nudities" (Codeluppi 2013: 149). In the next sections, we will look in further detail at the creative and symbolic overlapping between advertising, television, and cinema.

2.3 It's not (only) RAI: the Italian television duopoly

The 30-year period dealt with in this chapter definitively consecrated television as the single most influential medium of Italian society. Between the 1980s and the 2000s, television was able to absorb half of the advertising resources available on the market, thus leaving press, radio, and all the other media to share the crumbs (Brigida, Baudi Di Vesme, and Francia 2004). Television was the launch pad from which Silvio Berlusconi's career started, as well as the stage on which most of Italy's subsequent political events have unfolded. More broadly, over those years, television introduced and popularised a new aesthetic model that was able to penetrate all other major forms of Italian cultural production. Television did so, or rather, to use Umberto Eco's words, *Neo-Television* (1990) did. Eco used the term Neo-Television to describe a new way of conceiving, producing, programming, and consuming television contents that took hold in the 1980s following the arrival of private commercial channels and of new devices such as the remote control. Among the characteristics that Eco (1990: 246–247) attributed to Neo-TV and that influenced the entire Italian media landscape in the years to come were a marked self-reference ("Whereas Paleo-TV talked about the external world, or pretended to, Neo-Television talks about itself and about the contact that it establishes with its own public") and a hybridisation of the traditionally separated genres of information, culture, and entertainment ("The 'hold-all' programme has arrived in which, maybe for several hours, a host talks, plays music, introduces a drama programme and perhaps a documentary or a debate, and even reads the news"). Neo-Television was epitomised by Berlusconi's Fininvest and contrasted *Paleo-Television*, which was instead represented by the RAI of the now-extinct public monopoly. Indeed, newness became a key selling point of Fininvest in the heated competition with RAI for audience ratings. Fininvest framed the competition with RAI as an ideological battle between two opposed lifestyles that Italian viewers had to buy into: on the one hand, there was private television—fresh, friendly, and liberal—whereas on the other hand there was the old, authoritative, and prudish public service broadcaster. Perhaps the most telling symbol of this opposed view of television, and society, lays in an entertainment show turned cult, aired by Fininvest/Mediaset between 1991 and 1995, and titled *Non è la RAI* ("It's not RAI"). *Non è la RAI* was a 90-minute-long live afternoon show where a group of teenage girls, as young as 14, played games, danced, and lip-synced on a beach-like studio set, while constantly smiling to the camera. The programme was designed to appeal simultaneously to a female teen and pre-teen audience, who saw the girls on screen, with their looks and their slang, as trendy role models, and to appeal to a slightly older male audience, to whom the broadcaster winked by giving the show an underlying sexual connotation. The first two seasons of the programme were presented by Enrica Bonaccorti, who had previously been one of RAI's signature talents, whereas the final ones were presented by one of the girls, Ambra Angiolini, who later became one of the most famous faces of Italian cinema.

The television anomaly

The 1975 Reform Law had reaffirmed RAI's status as a public monopoly, whilst also introducing changes to the organisation and governance that were

46 *The normalisation of anomaly*

supposed to improve its performance in terms of political pluralism. As we have seen, the result was in fact one of increased political control over its three channels, split between the main national parties. In 1976, referencing RAI's poor record of political fairness, and the greater frequency capacity brought by technological advancements, the Italian Constitutional Court stated the legitimacy of private terrestrial broadcasting at the local level. With this historic sentence (n. 202/1976), which came after a decade-long series of judicial battles, the last brick that kept the wall of the public radio and television monopoly standing was lost. What followed was a flourishing across the peninsula of both privately owned and community radio and television stations that sustained themselves through local advertising. Some companies bypassed the court's decision by transmitting the same videotaped programmes from different local stations at slightly shifted times, thus providing, in effect, a nationwide private television service. Among them, there was Fininvest that, between 1982 and 1984, had incorporated the networks of its main competitors (publishing houses turned media companies Rusconi and Mondadori), thus creating a "virtual private monopoly controlled by the Berlusconi group" (Richeri 1990: 257). Berlusconi's political connection to then Socialist Prime Minister Bettino Craxi was instrumental in allowing him to grow his media empire: until 1985, under the provision of three ad hoc decrees, and afterwards, thanks to a prolonged regulatory vacuum. In 1984, the Italian broadcasting landscape appeared as a duopoly: the public service broadcaster controlled three channels (RAI 1, RAI 2, RAI 3), just like the private competitor Fininvest (Canale 5, Italia 1, Rete 4). The lack of appropriate regulatory measures—also due to the government's unwillingness to obstruct Berlusconi's ascent—made the advent of commercial broadcasting in Italy a case of "savage deregulation" (Hallin and Mancini 2004: 125). For such reasons, the 1980s has become known as the "Wild West" of Italian broadcasting history (Hibberd 2008: 77).

The Italian "Wild West" eventually ended in 1990, when the *pentapartito* government issued the Mammì law (Law 6 August 1990, n. 223), so-called after the Minister of Communications who proposed it. As to the legal position of the players in the market, and especially Fininvest, which had been operating on the basis of an expired parliamentary concession, the Mammì law basically confirmed the status quo. The public broadcaster's monopoly over national terrestrial television officially ended, and the private competitor secured the ground for the growth into the next decade. The Mammì law also transposed parts of the provisions included in the first Europewide directive concerning the audiovisual industry: Television Without Frontiers (TVWF) (Directive 89/552/EEC). The TVWF Directive aimed to create and protect an internal market for European audiovisual works and to set minimum standards for safeguarding public interest objectives. As a

The normalisation of anomaly 47

result of the directive, private commercial televisions, such as Berlusconi's Canale 5, Italia 1, and Rete 4, had to devote a majority of its programming time to Europe-made content and to start transmitting news programmes.

In terms of ownership and market structure, the 1990s opened for Italian television along very similar lines as the previous decade: there was an "imperfect duopoly" (Ortoleva 2008: 98) constituted, on the one hand, by the three channels of the public service broadcaster and, on the other hand, by those of Berlusconi's group. In December 1994, a new judgement by the Italian Constitutional Court found parts of the Mammì law incompatible with anti-concentration laws and urged the Parliament to issue a new regulation. This had become an ever-pressing political matter, as Berlusconi had, in the meantime, been elected prime minister. In such a context, therefore, an anti-concentration law would have also been a law against the conflict of interest of Italy's most powerful politician. A first attempt at solving this situation came in 1997, when the centre-left government led by Romano Prodi issued the "Maccanico law" (n. 2497/1997), from the name of its proponent. The Maccanico law established an independent Authority for Communications Guarantees (AGCOM), with the aim of supervising and regulating competition in the communications sector. The law also established new anti-concentration thresholds: a single operator could not control more than 30 per cent of total television market resources or more than 20 per cent of total communication resources (i.e. press, radio, and television). According to these provisions, Mediaset should have transferred one of its networks to the satellite and RAI should have broadcast one of its networks without advertising. These were unwanted consequences for Berlusconi's party and allies, but also for the left-wing political forces that, thanks to the system of *lottizzazione*, controlled RAI's third channel. Therefore, the anti-concentration provisions of the Maccanico law were never implemented. Meanwhile, governments changed hands, and the prospect of digital switchover put any further attempts at solving the Italian television anomaly on hold.

At the turn of the 2000s, the Italian market for analogue terrestrial television had already been living for over 20 years in a sort of permanent transitional state, with missing laws, unenforced laws, and laws contradicted by judicial interventions. In the meantime, new players had been entering the market. In 2003, Australian American media mogul Rupert Murdoch landed in Italy to launch satellite television Sky Italia: this incorporated the two national pay TV companies Tele+ and Stream TV, which had been operating, with limited success, since 1991 and 1997 respectively. Also in 2003, another international player, Discovery Channel, opened an Italian branch: Discovery Italia. At the end of the 2000s, the Italian television market comprised five main actors: RAI, Mediaset, Sky Italia, Discovery Italia, and La7, the latter being a free-to-air channel created from the former

48 *The normalisation of anomaly*

Tele Monte Carlo (TMC), the Italian language television channel from the Principality of Monaco. The arrival of new players, though, did not bring significant improvements in terms of market concentration, which is still very high in 2016, according to the international measure of the Herfindahl-Hirschman index (AGCOM 2017). The lack of improvement in this area is largely due to a third law reforming the television system, which passed in 2004 under Berlusconi's second government, and is currently still in force. Law No. 112 of 2004, named the Gasparri law after the then Minister of Communications, should have solved the long-overdue issue of market concentration, as well as regulated the switch over to digital terrestrial television. The passing of the Gasparri law was unusually long and extremely controversial. The main point of contention was the introduction of an unprecedentedly broad base for the calculation of anti-concentration thresholds, which was not limited to advertising revenues generated from the television sector, but it also included those from print media, radio, cinema, and Internet (the "Integrated system of communication", SIC). As a result of this provision, the anti-concentration caps on advertising revenues were actually raised from 12 to 26 billion euros (Leonida, Maimone Ansaldo Patti, and Navarra 2015: 268), thus effectively safeguarding Berlusconi's media group from any risk of downsizing. Moreover, the Gasparri law established an unrealistic deadline for the digital switchover, December 31, 2006 (which in fact occurred six years later), thus refraining from regulating the allocation of frequencies for analogue terrestrial television. Once again, Italian policymakers did not solve the television anomaly, in fact, they institutionalised it for reasons of political calculus, on the part of the right-wing government and, for political inability, on the part of the left-wing opposition.

Advertising is king

The demise of the public service monopoly and the chaotic rise of commercial television that ensued had an explosive effect on the Italian advertising market. Under the monopoly, advertising spaces were limited and only a relatively small group of companies could afford the large investments needed to create films that would meet RAI's strict directives and that would only be aired twice. Following deregulation, dozens of small- and medium-sized enterprises that had previously been excluded from this market started investing in television advertising. The result was a rapid and massive growth in advertising investments, which went from 0.33 per cent of Italy's GDP in 1981 to 0.63 per cent in 1990 (Brigida, Baudi Di Vesme, and Francia 2004: 21). Moreover, there was also a remarkable shift in advertising budgets across the Italian media system. In the space of a decade, television absorbed large portions of the advertising investments that

Table 2.1 Percentage distribution of advertising resources in the 1980s

	Television	Press	Radio	Cinema	Outdoor
1980	25.7	59.0	6.7	1.9	6.7
1981	30.1	56.5	5.6	1.3	6.5
1982	36.2	52.0	5.2	0.7	5.9
1983	42.8	46.0	4.9	0.5	5.8
1984	47.3	43.1	3.9	0.2	5.5
1985	48.7	42.3	3.6	0.2	5.2
1986	47.6	43.5	3.6	0.3	5.0
1987	46.9	44.1	3.6	0.3	5.1
1988	47.5	43.8	3.5	0.4	4.8
1989	46.7	44.6	3.7	0.3	4.7
1990	47.9	43.7	3.6	0.3	4.5

Source: Brigida, F., P. Baudi Di Vesme, and L. Francia, 2004, *Media e pubblicità in Italia*, 3rd edition, Franco Angeli, p. 24.

were previously allocated elsewhere (Table 2.1). For the first time in 1983, Berlusconi's networks overtook the public service broadcaster in advertising revenues (45.5 versus 34.6 per cent), and, by the end of the decade, it had doubled it (60.1 versus 31.8 per cent) (Brigida, Baudi Di Vesme, and Francia 2004: 21).

The growth in advertising investment, though, was not simply due to a multiplication of the spaces available. It was also the result of a radically different way of understanding the television medium with particular regard to its relationship with the major stakeholders of advertisers, on the one hand, and viewers, on the other. Berlusconi understood that, unlike public service broadcasting, the core business of commercial television did not lie in the creation and transmission of content to be consumed by an audience. Quite the opposite: the aim of commercial television was to create, package, and sell viewers to advertisers. This was, if we may say so, the "Copernican revolution" brought by Neo-Television, where all editorial decisions were aiming towards maximisation and segmentation of the audience to the benefit of the networks' clients, i.e. the advertisers. As Forgacs (2000) observed:

> (I)t was the advertising sales company that decided the content of a programme, on the basis of the interest it might raise in the advertisers, and not the broadcaster, on the basis of some cultural policy, or of an insight into the needs or tastes of the audience.
>
> (p. 278, my translation)

In line with this logic, advertising was no longer confined within the times of individual programmes, but instead it was broken down into smaller

50   *The normalisation of anomaly*

parts (spots of initially 60 seconds, then 30 and 15 seconds) and broadcast back-to-back multiple times per day. RAI started to programme spot advertising right after the demise of the *Carosello* format in 1977. Initially, RAI broadcast eight advertising "blocks", right before and after the most important programmes of the day. These blocks opened and closed to an animated interstitial, which marked the separation of advertising from "regular" programmes.[6] Besides the public service broadcaster, advertising spots were already an integral part of the programming of the dozens of local commercial TV stations that started to appear across the country in the late 1970s. Commercial televisions soon started to expand advertising formats, by programming *televendite* (teleshopping) and, since the mid-1980s, *telepromozioni* ("telepromotions").[7] The content offer of commercial television reflected its will to meet the advertisers' needs. Entertainment was the predominant genre, with a massive use of content imported from abroad: Latin American *telenovelas*, Japanese cartoons, and, above all, US-made serial programmes, such as soap operas and sitcoms. The massive import of US-made fiction during the 1980s was not exclusive of Italian television. In Italy, though, this phenomenon was more pronounced and extended in time, compared to other EU countries, as still in 1997, Italian commercial televisions were devoting 73 per cent of their prime-time airtime to US-made fiction (against 52.7 per cent in France, 69.2 in Germany, and 33.4 in Great Britain) (De Bens and De Smaele 2001: 56). As Monteleone (1992) observed, "after so many years, the American model still determined the choices of Italian television" (p. 449). These types of shows were programmed not only because they were cheap and pre-tested successful formats, but also because, being serialised narrations, they fostered loyal, repeating viewing on the part of the viewers/consumers. The scheduling of advertising breaks followed the suspense peaks of the narrations, so as to minimise the risk of viewers changing channel and missing the commercials. Moreover, the original programmes produced by Berlusconi's networks were conceived and structured from the beginning as a sequence of fast-paced, self-contained frames. In this way, not only could they incorporate advertising breaks more organically, but they also came to resemble advertisements themselves (to this regard, an analysis of Fininvest's popular variety show *Drive In* can be found in Grasso 2000).

The popularity of the newborn commercial television started to be certified by official data in 1984 when Auditel was established. Auditel is a limited liability company that collects and publishes daily data on TV viewing ratings. It was founded on the joint initiative of broadcasters and advertisers with the aim of obtaining impartial and reliable data that were to be used to set the price list of television advertising. Auditel's main shareholders are RAI, Mediaset, and the industry bodies representing Italian advertisers

The normalisation of anomaly 51

(UPA) and advertising agencies (Assocom). Since its founding, Auditel has been collecting data from channels operating through the whole spectrum of digital terrestrial and cable as well as satellite. However, with the progressive broadening and fragmenting of the Italian mediascape, Auditel has been the object of concern about possible conflicts of interests stemming from its ownership structure. Sky Italia, for example, has repeatedly lamented unfair treatment on the part of Auditel, which effectively is still controlled by the duopolists of the Italian TV market.

The arrival of Auditel had a disruptive impact on the quality of television programming in Italy in the 1980s and onwards. Faced with unprecedented challenges, RAI started to make poor editorial decisions in the attempt to compete with Berlusconi's networks on the latter's favourite terrain: entertainment (Monteleone 1992). RAI reduced educational and cultural programmes in favour of light entertainment, talk shows, and infotainment. Even RAI's news programmes started to incorporate elements of the American news model, based on a charismatic anchorman, as well as the sensationalism typical of the British tabloid model. Mediaset adopted such style since its very first live news programme aired on January 16, 1991, which opened to journalist Emilio Fede frantically announcing the break of the Gulf War, banging his fist on the desk to the words "They have attacked!" Following Auditel's introduction, RAI and Fininvest entered a scheduling and counter-scheduling battle that resulted in an overall discount of the quality of television programming of the time. Italian commentators and policymakers were aware of this issue from an early stage. In October 1988, during a meeting of the Senate Commission on Communications, the representative of the Italian Association of Radio and Television Listeners (AIART) stated that "the idolatry of the ratings, which have become the fetishes of our modern civilization of images (causes) a flattening, a homologation to low levels, a banality and also vulgarity of the programmes" (my translation from original Italian, Senato della Repubblica 1988). Moreover, the battle of the ratings brought to light the conflicts inherent to RAI's mixed revenue model of annual fee and advertising. After the end of the monopoly, RAI found itself unprepared to face the competition with commercial television. Berlusconi's channels pursued an aggressive policy for audience maximisation, which included the buyout of talents traditionally associated to the public service broadcaster. In such an unprecedented situation, RAI made some poor editorial decisions, trying to chase commercial programming in a way that contrasted with its original mission, and, ultimately, with its very identity as a public service broadcaster. Such issues continued into the following decades and are, to a large extent, unresolved still today. Since the 1980s, the Italian television scene has evolved, and one key aspect has intensified: the centrality of entertainment as a communication genre,

52 *The normalisation of anomaly*

style, and language. As Umberto Eco observed, it is during those years that "the philosophy of entertainment programs has inevitably set to become the philosophy of television as a whole" (quoted in Monteleone 1992: 463).

2.4 Italian cinema between advertising, television, and the state

In the 1980s, the symbolic as well as economic relationship that had been connecting cinema, television, and advertising in Italy since *Carosello* started growing increasingly close to the point of becoming a "symbiotic mechanism", whereby "as years go by, one takes the features of the other" (Pitteri 2006: 172). One the most powerful and effective representations of such phenomenon can be found in the film *The Icicle Thief* ("Ladri di saponette" 1989), directed by Maurizio Nichetti, who also plays himself in the leading role. The film, characterised by the mimicry and surreal tone that are typical of its author—once nicknamed by an Italian film critic as "the Buster Keaton of Lombardy"—opens to a long take of Nichetti who arrives at the studios of a commercial television, where his latest film, a black-and-white, Neorealism-inspired drama, is about to be broadcast as a part of an arthouse film screenings series. The chatty studio assistant who welcomes Nichetti promptly informs him that the film series is performing very well, with TV ratings up to 8 million viewers. Shortly after, *The Icicle Thief*'s editing becomes frantic, and frames of a tennis game, a fitness show, and a jewellery telepromotion appear, as the camera shows us a little girl playing with the TV remote on the couch of her family's living room. The situation is that of a typical middle-class Italian family, past dinner time: the mother complains to her husband for not letting her watch her favourite US soap opera; the father distractedly glances at the TV screen while leafing through a newspaper; the eldest son sits on the carpet in front of the TV and plays noisily with a pile of Lego bricks; the only one paying attention to Nichetti's film is the little girl, to whom a harsh Neorealist film should not actually be shown. The sequence set at the TV studio and the one set at the family's apartment contrast sharply. The former, stages the conflicts arising from a commercial television using a motion picture as a mere carrier for advertisement: "Of course I'm complaining"—Nichetti snaps to the studio assistant after seeing one of his film character's line being cut mid-sentence by advertising—"It's time to address more seriously the problem of advertising interruptions during films and we need to have more respect for the work of others!" On the other hand, the household sequence shows the impact that such treatment has on the audience's perception of—even socially committed Neorealist—cinema, which becomes undistinguishable from the rest of the loud flow of images that comes out of

The normalisation of anomaly 53

the TV screen (much like the hundreds of Lego bricks that the boy spreads out in front of the TV set). *The Icicle Thief* pushes such argument to a surreal extreme when it shows that, following a power failure in the studio, the full-colour characters populating the commercials end up in the black-and-white scenes of the film they were interrupting. The outcome is a peculiar, self-reflective, and post-modernist parody that, whilst entertaining for the viewer, also speaks seriously to the love-and-hate relationship that linked Italian cinema, television, and advertising of the time.

You don't interrupt an emotion!

In previous pages we mentioned the fact that, since the 1980s, the exchanges and mutual influences between Italian cinema, television, and advertising have grown increasingly systematic, both in terms of the language and style of the communication, and in terms of the talents employed. Some of the most important Italian filmmakers have directed spots or entire campaigns for various national brands. For example, Franco Zeffirelli directed French star Alain Delon and a young Monica Bellucci in a spot for fur brand Annabella (1984); Giuseppe Tornatore directed the commercials for luxury clothing brand Dolce & Gabbana since 1994 (also starring model and actress Monica Bellucci); Daniele Luchetti directed many spots, starting from one for dairy products brand Danone in 1993; even Maurizio Nichetti, who, as we have seen, took a critical stance towards television advertising in *The Icicle Thief*, had a long career as director of popular *Carosello* and TV commercials (over a hundred between 1974 and 2001). Indeed, what Maurizio Nichetti was critical of was not so much advertising itself, as it was the way in which commercial televisions were airing advertising, at the expense, in particular, of motion pictures. Nichetti shared the same stance as hundreds of other Italian filmmakers, actors and actresses, screenwriters, and film professionals who got together to protest advertising breaks during films: among them, Marcello Mastroianni, Ettore Scola, Roberto Benigni, Suso Cecchi D'Amico, Gillo Pontecorvo, and the Taviani brothers. The filmmakers' protest found a distinguished and passionate spokesperson in Federico Fellini, who created the slogan "You don't interrupt an emotion" (*Non si interrompe un'emozione*). Fellini, who had also directed TV commercials (for Campari liqueur in 1984 and Barilla pasta in 1985), launched an anti-interruptions campaign that went on for a whole decade, even after his death. In 1985, the director of *La Dolce Vita* sued Silvio Berlusconi's Canale 5 for alleged moral rights infringement. Advertising breaks, Fellini claimed, not only damaged the rhythm and overall quality of his films, but, by doing so, they also harmed the director's artistic reputation. In July 1985, though, the Italian magistrate rejected Fellini's claim. Despite disapproving

54 *The normalisation of anomaly*

the alteration to the film's narrative flow caused by the interruptions, the magistrate decided that no real harm had been caused, as Italian viewers were by then used to commercial breaks during films (*LaRepubblica* 1985). Five years later, the first comprehensive Italian law on public and private broadcasting, the 1990 Mammì Law, introduced hourly caps to advertising programming (12 per cent for the public service broadcaster; 18 per cent for commercial networks), but allowed up to four advertising breaks during 90-minute-long films, and up to five interruptions for films longer than 110 minutes (Law 223/1990, Article 8, Point 3).

In 1995, two years after Fellini's passing, Italian left-wing parties, and especially the Partito Democratico della Sinistra (PDS; "Democratic Party of the Left", to a large extent the heir of the Italian Communist Party) launched a referendum that asked voters to repeal that provision of the Mammì law and completely ban advertising during films. The referendum campaign was managed by Walter Veltroni, the then head of PDS' propaganda and information commission, as well as future minister for Cultural Heritage and two-times mayor of Rome. Veltroni—who is now retired from active political life and has become a documentary filmmaker himself—decided to adopt Fellini's "You don't interrupt an emotion" slogan in support of the referendum. The anti-advertising campaign was opposed by both Socialists and right-wing parties, who presented it as the dusty legacy of a vision of society that the demise of the public service monopoly had made permanently outdated. Berlusconi's networks replied to the referendum by appropriating one of the slogans of the 1968 leftist uprising: "Forbidden to forbid" (*Vietato vietare*) (Minuz 2015a: 163). As it had happened in the past (see Chapter 1, section "Advertising modernity"), the politically driven discourse around advertising got polarised between a framing of advertising as a symbol of modernity and freedom, on the one hand, and as advertising regulation as an expression of backwardness and state censorship, on the other. Such discourse, whilst reductionist, found favourable ground in the cultural climate of 1990s Italy, which, as previously described, was largely rejecting the political establishment to embrace a more individualistic and post-ideologic view of society. In June 1995, the majority of Italian voters rejected the anti-advertising referendum with a 10 per cent gap. It was a "castigation of the state broadcaster and political parties with their traditional view of television" and "an indication of how much things had changed" (Minuz 2015a: 163).

Advertising breaks during films were not an Italian exception, as the limits imposed by the Mammì law reflected similar ones set by the Television Without Frontier Directive for all European countries. However, in the Italian case, the clash between the most liberal positions, who favoured advertising breaks during films, and the most protectionist ones, who wanted to see it banned, was loaded with further political and ideological significance,

The normalisation of anomaly 55

which derived from the country's television anomaly. In Italy, one major right-wing politician not only owned the quasi-monopoly of private broadcasting and the dominant advertising enterprise (Publitalia), but, because of the *lottizzazione* system, Berlusconi could also control the governance and editorial line of the public service broadcaster as prime minister (which he has been four times between 1994 and 2011). This circumstance has led to the traditional opposition between arthouse and commercial cinema, to take on Italian-specific ideological political connotations, which emerged clearly during the 1995 referendum. Advertising, which had already been part of the Italian audiovisual media system during the public service monopoly, came to be ultimately identified with Berlusconi's economic and political power. Advertising and television thus became associated with Berlusconi's right-wing populist politics, whereas Italian cinema became a byword for left-wing, anti-Berlusconi positions (so-called Berlusconism and anti-Berlusconism).

For the Italian film industry, such context produced two main consequences, which, as we shall in see in further detail over the next sections, still endures today. Firstly, it politicised, in Italian-specific terms, the universal distinction between highbrow (and even middlebrow) culture, on the one hand, and lowbrow productions, on the other. Italian contemporary highbrow cinema is represented by award-winning, internationally renowned auteurs such as Matteo Garrone, Luca Guadagnino, Paolo Sorrentino, and Nanni Moretti. All of these auteurs have commented, through very diverse stories and styles, on the Italian political and social climate, and they have also expressed their left-wing political positions publicly. In fact, Sorrentino and Moretti explicitly thematised Italian politics, and the figure of Silvio Berlusconi in particular, in two of their films: respectively *Loro* act 1 and *Loro* act 2 ("Them", 2018), and *April* (1998) and *The Caiman* (2006). Italian middlebrow cinema is represented by a wide range of filmmakers, whose popularity remains mostly confined within the national borders. Examples include Paolo Virzì, Ferzan Ozpetek, Michele Placido, and Alessandro D'Alatri, who, despite often dealing with social and political issues, do so "through the charismatic seal of a light authorial touch, one which is not prominent, nor exclusive" (Menarini 2010: 42, my translation from original Italian). Paolo Virzì, in particular, directed the comedy *August Vacation* (*Ferie d'agosto*, 1996), which represented in an ironic but effective way how the choices on cultural consumption and entertainment made by parts of the Italian society of the time reflected specific political affiliations. *August Vacation* tells the story of two separate groups of family and friends who occupy adjacent holiday houses in the isle of Ventotene. One group is made of anti-Berlusconi environmentalists, who live without electricity and despise television; the other group cannot live without watching

56 *The normalisation of anomaly*

television (the teenage daughter is glued to *Non è la RAI*), and mocks the Italian left-wing intellectuals, embodied by their neighbours, for "not understanding shit, and since a very long time". The film was shot one year after Berlusconi's first surprising election and captured very well the cultural and political divide that his victory sparked within Italian society. On the opposite end of the cultural and political spectrum, Italian lowbrow cinema is essentially represented by the comedy genre of *cinepanettoni*. Critics and scholars have repeatedly highlighted the ideological closeness between the genre of cinepanettoni and the Berlusconism. As we have already partly pointed out, these two had in common the celebration of a consumerist, individualist and post-ideological culture, and the communication of contents of a strongly populist nature. In addition, the cinepanettoni often used comedians and personalities of television origin. The popularity of Berlusconism and that of cinepanettoni also followed similar trajectories, to the point that journalist Curzio Maltese, in commenting on the disappointing box office performance of the 2011 instalment of this genre, *Vacanze di Natale a Cortina* ("Christmas holidays in Cortina"), wrote: "It is perhaps the first and most sensational sign of the end of the Berlusconi era. The cinepanettone is to the twenty-year Berlusconian period what the white-telephone films were to the twenty-year fascist period" (Maltese 2011).[8]

The television anomaly also produced a second important consequence for the relationship between the Italian film and advertising industry: it has led to a resistance on the part of Italian filmmakers to collaborate with advertisers and, even when they do, to publicly acknowledge it. Television advertising thus came to be considered as a second-class form of creative work. While *Carosello* was a highly respected form of audiovisual production—which, as previously mentioned, even an intransigent auteur like Jean-Luc Godard had praised—television advertising during the Berlusconism became a controversial way for a filmmakers to employ their talent. Nanni Moretti provided an ironic representation of such conceptualisation in a sequence of his film *April* (1998), which chronicles the two years following Berlusconi's first electoral win. Frustrated by the inability of the left-wing parties to rebut Berlusconi's election campaign, Moretti, who plays himself in the film, gets into the car and goes in search of someone to argue with. Suddenly, he remembers that his friend and former assistant Daniele Luchetti is shooting a pasta commercial and joins him on set with the intention of provoking him:

Moretti: "Now, I don't understand the reason why you should be doing commercials…"

Luchetti: "There's nothing unusual in it. There's plenty of filmmakers, even important ones, who, once in a while, do commercials: Lynch, Polanski, Ridley Scott, Kiarostami…"

Moretti:	"Actually, Kiarostami never did commercials."
Luchetti:	"But Fellini did! Woody Allen did!"
Moretti:	"Yes, yes they did. Ok, I'll shut up…"

In justifying his choice as a filmmaker to work on advertising, Daniele Luchetti references the examples of important (and mainly foreign) auteurs, which forces Moretti to reluctantly give up his argument. This sort of double-standard view that advertising/television commercials are respectful audiovisual works for filmmakers abroad but not so much so for Italian ones derives from the peculiar ideological and political connotation that television (and advertising with it) has for Italian film auteurs: they are inextricably associated to Berlusconism. In the next chapter, we will see how this double standard still applies and how it has influenced the implementation of new integrated form of commercials communications: product placement and branded entertainment.

This film is brought to you by

In terms of cinema attendance, the period covered by this chapter marked an all-time negative record. After the boom of the mid 1950s, theatrical admissions had been declining progressively but incessantly through the following decades. In 1980, the number of admissions to Italian cinemas was of 241.8 million people. At the turn of the 1990s, this figure dropped of 62.5 per cent and 1992 marked an all-time negative record of 83.5 million admissions (Corsi 2003). Film scholars have traced Italians' apparent disaffection for moviegoing back to a general crisis in national film production, which emerged in terms of smaller numbers of yearly production, as well as in terms of their quality, despite some remarkable exceptions. Indeed, between 1989 and 1992, two Italian pictures won the Academy Award for Best Foreign Language Film: Giuseppe Tornatore's *Cinema Paradiso* and Gabriele Salvatores' *Mediterraneo*. It is interesting to note, though, that both of these films, just like Roberto Benigni's *Life Is Beautiful*, which also won the same award in 1998, were set in the past and notably during a time frame that goes from the start of World War II to the early post-war period. This seems to suggest that the creative crisis of Italian cinema over the 1980s and 1990s was at least partly due to the filmmakers' difficulty in looking at, and commenting on, the present time. Such difficulty can be ascribed to the broader crisis that Italian left-wing intellectuals were experiencing as a result of the cultural and political transformations that were happening within the society at the time. Moreover, scholars have also associated Italy's negative trend in film admissions to the rise in the country of domestic forms of film consumption. The advent of commercial

58 *The normalisation of anomaly*

television had multiplied the offer of film programming available to viewers (although, as previously discussed, televised films were often "butchered" by frequent and reckless advertising breaks). Also, in the 1980s Italian households started adopting home video sets, which allowed them to record and store films for domestic consumption. As Italian film scholar Gian Piero Brunetta observed, "From a certain point on, Italian cinema seemed to mean a television product, and American cinema meant a film product" (Brunetta 2003: 736, my translation from original Italian). Since the 1980s, television became for Italian families what cinema had been 30 years earlier: the privileged form of popular entertainment.

The 1980s and 1990s were the years when the financing system of Italian cinema took shape, which will remain dominant, albeit with some modifications, until today. This system rests on two main pillars: the Italian state and the national broadcasters. With regard to the funds provided by the state, in 1985 Law No. 163 of April 30, 1985, established the creation of the FUS (*Fondo Unico per lo spettacolo*, "Single fund for the performing arts"), which centralised in a single fund the resources previously distributed to cinema but also to other national arts (opera, prose theatre, music, dance, and circus) through other instruments. The FUS is administered by the Ministry of Cultural Heritage & Activities and Tourism (MiBACT) and its financial endowment is determined each year by the national budget law. The distribution of FUS funding across the different arts follows different percentages, which are adjusted from one year to the other, to conform with possible fluctuating needs on the part of the sectors concerned: in 1985, the overall endowment of the FUS corresponded to around 0.84 per cent of the Italian GDP, with one quarter of funds going to the film sector. However, this also meant that industry operators could not rely on the same overall budget from one year to the next. Since its founding, the FUS has been the main source of funding for Italian film producers, who could apply before starting production, by submitting the film's script. A dedicated commission of film experts, chosen by political appointment, evaluated the scripts and adjudicated the funds on the basis of the "cultural interest" criterion.[9] The biggest part of the FUS funding that each producer received was direct and non-repayable, i.e. the producer was obliged to return only a small part of the funds, under penalty of exclusion from the award of funds for three consecutive years. The FUS also provided for a system of indirect funding, in the form of tax breaks for companies operating in all phases of the film industry, but these were still comparably less attractive than the direct ones awarded through the cultural interest criterion (see Article 7 Law 163/1985). On the one hand, the FUS scheme of direct funding guaranteed a good degree of security and stability to the national film production, but, on the other hand, it also continued that system of "economic welfarism and

The normalisation of anomaly   59

political control" (Corsi 2001: 50–51) that had been going on since, and even before, the 1949 Andreotti law. As a result, a vast majority of Italian film production companies only lived for the time span of one title, whereas much fewer managed to sustain an average of one film production per year (respectively 155 and 13 between 1990 and 1998, according to Montanari and Usai, 2002: 58). Moreover, a study has showed that of all the public funds awarded between 1994 and 2002 through the cultural interest criterion, a stunning 85 per cent were not repaid (Tomasi 2004: 37).

The second pillar for national film funding is constituted by television. In 1989, the European TVWF Directive made it mandatory (albeit providing some space for waivers) for public as well as private broadcasters operating in member states to devote the majority of their scheduling time to programmes produced by European companies, as well as to invest at least 10 per cent of their programming budget in audiovisual works produced by European independent companies (i.e. not controlled by broadcasters). This provision proved essential for reinforcing the European audiovisual market in the face of the competition with US companies. In Italy, though, where the broadcasting market was abnormally concentrated around the imperfect duopoly of RAI and Fininvest/Mediaset, the TVWF Directive also meant that the effects of the television anomaly spilled over into the film industry. Thus, since the turn of the 1990s, the three top financiers of Italian film production have been the Italian state (by means of the MiBACT and the regional film commissions); the public service broadcaster through its affiliate RAI Cinema; and Silvio Berlusconi's commercial broadcaster, through its cinema branch, Medusa Film (Holdaway 2017). RAI and Mediaset have played a central role not only in the production phase of recent and contemporary Italian cinema, but also in the distribution phase, through their respective subsidiaries, 01 Distribution and Medusa. In fact, RAI and Mediaset are the only production companies in Italy to have a vertically integrated structure, which is essential to guarantee a market outlet to their films. The significant dependence of Italian film producers from broadcasters not only constitutes a drawback for the economic soundness and stability of their businesses, but it may also undermine the quality and specificity of their creative work. It is, in other words, a potential source of collaboration as well as a potential threat (Cigognetti and Sorlin 2007). The threat derives from the different logics at play when a film is conceived and produced primarily for theatrical release, or conversely for television broadcasting. These logics respond to the needs of radically different stakeholders: ticket-paying filmgoers in the former case, and advertisers in the latter.

Until the early 2000s, the ability of advertisers to influence the artistic choices and production strategies of Italian producers was potentially very strong, but still indirect. Things began to change in the 2000s when the

60 *The normalisation of anomaly*

Italian government started to issue a series of laws and policy measures aiming to transform in unprecedented ways the system of public funding of the national film industry. These changes were introduced between 2004 and 2010, and resulted in a new regulatory framework, which was characterised by two major aspects: first, a strong shift from direct to indirect state funding, namely through the provision of unprecedented and very appealing tax breaks for film investors; second, an openness to advertisers as new key players for the film production industry, notably through the provision of new, dedicated policy measures (product placement and tax credit for non-audiovisual companies). These aspects contributed to shift the focus of the overall Italian policymaking philosophy, in favour of a marketisation of national film production. In the next chapter we will look in detail at the regulatory framework of product placement and tax credit for non-audiovisual companies. We will consider how such a framework impacts the production strategies and the creative output of Italian film companies, as well as how the Italian cinema marketisation trend, which the product placement and tax credit policies have contributed to accelerate, had continued through the most recent cinema reform law, approved in 2016. In doing so, we will also present the voices and experiences of Italian film and marketing professionals on the subject.

Notes

1 From the very beginning, Italian newspapers and televisions reported about the Bribesgate investigation with oversensationalist tones, publishing names, leaking confidential information, and often without making distinctions between politicians who were simply indicted and those who were actually convicted of corruption crimes. Such a harsh mediatisation has been considered partly responsible for a series of suicides committed by high-profile entrepreneurs who were involved in the investigation.
2 In the Italian language, the phrase "entering the field" is football related. Berlusconi, who was also the owner of Italian premier league team A.C. Milan, often used football and sport-related metaphors in his political speeches. For an in-depth analysis of this topic, see Semino and Masci (1996).
3 The name of Berlusconi's party—*Forza Italia* ("Come on Italy")—came from a homonymous slogan used by the Christian Democracy during the 1987 election campaign. This is just one example of Berlusconi's ability to appropriate the language and communication gimmicks of his political opponents and turn them against them. He will do the same a few years later to campaign against a referendum proposed by the Communist Party to abolish advertising breaks during televised films.
4 The tagline "Milano da bere" was designed by Marco Mignani, the same creative mind who, a couple of years later, would come up with the Christian Democracy's slogan *Forza Italia*, soon taken on by Silvio Berlusconi as the name of his new political party.

The normalisation of anomaly 61

5 The taste that the Italian *paninari* had for British synth pop artists was passionate and, to some degree, mutual: in 1985, Milanese teenager Clizia Gurrado published the semi-autobiographical novel, and immediate sensation, *I Will Marry Simon Le Bon: Confessions of a 16 Year-Old Madly in Love with Duran Duran.* In 1986, British synth pop duo Pet Shop Boys released a B-side single track titled *Paninaro*, a homage to the Italian youth subculture.

6 For an in-depth discussion of the textual and industrial significance of interstitials, particularly in relation to British television, see Grainge (2011).

7 *Televendite* are independent programmes in which a presenter, often in loud, barker-like style, invites viewers to purchase the advertised products via dedicated telephone numbers; they were particularly common for local commercial TV stations. A *telepromozione*, on the other hand, is a moment within a regular show (usually quizzes and light entertainment programmes) where the show's presenter talks extensively about a product, sometimes in company of a representative of the sponsoring company. Such a presentation, sometimes coupled with a short sketch reflecting the tone and atmosphere of the program, may take place in the same studio stage where the programme is set or in a separate one.

8 White-telephone films (*film dei telefoni bianchi*) were "socially conservative films of the Fascist era representing well-to-do protagonists in a mise-en-scène that invariably included the status symbol of white telephones" (Burke 2017: xxiii). They became a byword for cinema of governmental propaganda.

9 The ministry awards the "cultural interest" to a film which is produced by an artistic and technical crew of predominantly Italian professionals, and which presents significant artistic and cultural qualities, in relation to its contents, and/ or its stylistic and technical characteristics.

3 The imperfect marketisation

Italian advertising and cinema
in the 2000s

3.1 (Branded) content is king

On the verge of the 2000s, a motto echoed in advertising agencies and media companies around the world: "Content is king", as Bill Gates famously stated in an article published in 1996 on the Microsoft website. What Gates meant, essentially, was that in the then nascent Internet market, the most successful companies would be those capable of offering original, informative, entertaining (hence potentially profitable) contents to their users. For advertisers, this entailed a shift in the way brands conceived the relationship with their target groups and, consequently, how they transposed this relationship in advertising practices. Advertising communication re-focused on the (supposed) needs, emotions, and beliefs of the consumer, rather than those of the brand. Lifestyle marketing, which was prominent in commercial communications during the 1980s and 1990s, gave way to so-called *engagement marketing* (Gambetti and Grignaffa 2010), whereby brands leveraged content, causes, and values that their target groups were genuinely interested in or passionate about. Brands engaged consumers more and more at an emotional level, with the aim of building around themselves communities of loyal and affectionate users, along the lines of the thousands of online fan communities surrounding music artists, films, TV series, etc. Brands that were successful in building such communities—among them Apple and Coca-Cola for global markets, Nutella for the Italian market—became *lovemarks*, a term coined by Kevin Roberts, former CEO worldwide of Saatchi & Saatchi (Roberts 2004), which became very popular in advertising industry discourse. Lovemark brands were trailblazers in the use of storytelling as a means to elicit emotional engagement and active participation from their users, a strategy that became common practice for virtually all consumer companies over the second half of the 2000s. "Every company is a media company" was the marketing mantra elaborated by *Financial Times* journalist-turned-blogger Tom Foremski (Di Mauro 2010). In reality, though, not

The imperfect marketisation 63

every company is truly a media company, so advertisers had to rely on the expertise of third parties to design, manage, and create engaging narrations, most often in audiovisual formats. The latter could be in the form of fully controlled original content, through branded entertainment, or they could consist in brand insertions within films and programmes created by others that were consistent with the advertiser's values, namely product placement. In both instances, promotional intermediaries were key players in the new market. The term "promotional intermediaries" (Davies 2013; Grainge and Johnson 2015) conflates a plurality of organisations and occupational fields, including admen and adwomen; publicists; marketing, branding, and creative consultants; press agents; and PR specialists. In the Italian market for branded content and product placement, promotional intermediaries are professionals who perform consultancy, brokerage, and management work for advertisers and film companies to enable and facilitate the often-complex relationship between these two partners. Promotional intermediaries are privileged sources to understand how the relationships between advertisers and film producers work and their main critical points. They are not, of course, unbiased witnesses; on the contrary, they are actors who contribute to a significant extent to shape the market and the sometimes-contradictory dynamics within it. In this chapter, we will report the voices of Italian promotional intermediaries, as well as film producers. Firstly, though, we will look at the technological, economic, and regulatory factors that enabled advertisers and film producers to engage in ever more systematic forms of collaborations.

3.2 Millennium bugs: Brands and films in times of disruptions

During the first decade of the 21st century, a series of technological, economic, and cultural changes hit the media and advertising sectors in Italy and worldwide. Some of these changes were structural in nature in that they stemmed from a transformation of the logic underpinning the system; others were supposed to be temporary but ended up having long-term and far-reaching effects on the whole media and advertising sector. Among the structural changes, the most significant one was certainly the rise of the Internet, and notably its social functionalities, introduced with Web 2.0. For advertisers, the rise of the Internet and social media led to a substantial shift in the allocation of their advertising budget across media. As Hardy (2013: 135) summarised: 'At a general level, the shift of audiences' media consumption to the Internet has meant that advertisers have followed, and allocated their spending accordingly.' This was true for countries like the UK where Internet take-up grew rapidly during the decade, but also in Italy where the spread of household Internet connections was slower: in 2010, 75 per cent of the population in

64   *The imperfect marketisation*

Table 3.1 National and local advertising revenues across media (data in million euros)

	2005	2006	2007	2008	2009	2010	2011	2012
Television	4264.16	4285.83	4420.48	4398.47	4024.15	4282.36	4102.70	3532.43
Radio	429.84	483.36	515.40	578.49	558.66	598.92	559.55	509.75
Newspapers	1711.79	1757.11	1834.93	1759.91	1500.67	1410.80	1353.06	1133.87
Magazines	1418.52	1473.45	1532.26	1722.72	1293.43	1351.88	1317.01	1101.02
Trade pubs.	879.33	840.72	815.29	819.26	647.23	502.81	276.55	194.69
Cinema	83.00	76.20	78.42	65.53	57.60	68.10	58.57	45.15
Outdoor	570.00	587.00	612.18	602.00	492.00	481.00	423.28	374.18
Online	138.00	489.00	687.00	819.00	817.53	1177.29	1578.40	1699.94
TOTAL	9494.64	9992.67	10,495.96	10,765.38	9391.27	9873.16	9669.12	8591.03

Source: AGCOM, 2013, "Autorità per le Garanzie nelle Comunicazioni. Osservatorio sulla Pubblicità: Prima edizione",

the UK had access to the Internet (Ofcom 2016: 178) against 51.3 per cent in Italy (ISTAT 2013). Indeed, as Table 3.1 shows, since the second half of the decade, advertising spending in Italy started to shift towards online media.

Over the eight years from 2005, all media platforms, except online, reported a significant loss of revenues. Cinema, whose decline as an advertising medium had started in the 1970s, came to represent only 0.5 per cent of the overall advertising revenues in 2012. Print media particularly suffered from the rise of the Internet, which rose from 138 million euros in 2005 to 1.6 billion in 2012, and was 2.2 billion euros (1.98 billion British pounds) in 2018. Television also lost revenues, though remaining steadily above 40 per cent of the total (AGCOM 2013).

In addition to the structural transformations brought by the rise of the Internet, another major cause of disruption for the media and advertising sectors in the 2000s was the 2007–2008 global financial crisis. After starting in the US with the crisis in the subprime mortgage market, and Lehman Brothers' highly mediatised bankruptcy, the financial crisis spurred a global economic downturn, which, in terms of severity, was compared to the 1929 Great Depression. The economic crisis caused the global advertising market to mark a 10.3 per cent decline in revenues between 2007 and 2009 (McKinsey and Company 2013: 7). At the global level, it took four years for advertising revenues to return to pre-2008 figures, driven by the Asian Pacific and the Latin American regions. The advertising market in North America had to wait until 2014 to regain what had been lost during the crisis, one year longer in Western Europe (McKinsey and Company 2013: 7). Italy, though, was among the Eurozone countries—the so-called PIIGS (Portugal, Ireland, Italy, Greece, Spain)—that also experienced a dramatic debt crisis which prolonged and intensified the economic and social consequences of the global recession. In Italy, advertising revenues started to decrease between 2008 and 2009 and, in fact, never returned to pre-crisis values. Advertising revenues in Italy accounted for overall 7.36 billion euros in 2017, with all media, except the Internet, on a declining curve (AGCOM 2018: 106). This means that, in the Italian case, what was supposed to be a temporary, if dramatic, form of disruption morphed into a structural and, so far, permanent trait of the national advertising market. In terms of advertising and marketing communications, this situation produced a twofold and apparently contradictory outcome: on the one hand, it pushed advertisers to invest even more in television, which they perceived as a "safe harbour" in times of economic and media disruptions; on the other hand, it made them want to experiment with less traditional and comparably cheaper marketing techniques, such as product placement and branded entertainment.

Beyond the advertising market, the prolonged economic crisis also had an impact on the Italian film sector, particularly because of the reduction in state funding for film production. The FUS (*Fondo Unico per lo spettacolo*) which traditionally provided the greatest share of direct public funding to Italian cinema and performing arts, got progressively cut down: 363.48 million euros in 1985, the year of its creation; 530.92 million euros in 2001, its highest endowment ever; 397.01 million euros in 2009, in the midst of the government debt crisis; and 333.72 million euros in 2017 (MIBAC 2017: 36). In such a persistent economic recession, Italian governments could no longer bear the costs of being the major provider of direct funding to the national film industry. Hence, from the mid-2000s onwards, Italian policymakers started implementing measures to encourage private actors to invest in the national film industry by providing them with both financial and promotional advantages. The economic crisis certainly played a major role in this, but Italian policymakers' decision was not solely born out of necessity. This is reflected, for example, in the fact that the FUS budget has not only decreased in absolute monetary value, but also in its relative value in relation to the national GDP: from 0.084 per cent in 1985 to 0.019 in 2017, an overall decrease of over 63 per cent in 32 years (MIBAC 2017: 36). What drove Italian policymakers' decision to implement such a new approach to film funding was the aim to encourage a broader cultural shift to push filmmakers and producers to develop a more market-oriented mindset (Dagnino 2014). However, as we will see later, a similar debate was also taking place at the level of the European Union (EU), which, in those same years, was about to update the legislative framework of the audiovisual industry.

3.3 Levelling the field? A new policy framework for brands and films

At the turn of the 2000s, the EU's audiovisual media policy framework was still largely based on the provisions set back in 1989 by the Television

66 *The imperfect marketisation*

Without Frontiers (TVWF) Directive. The directive was updated in 1997, but many policy areas had remained essentially unchanged: among them, advertising and commercial communications. The rise of digital technologies, and the altered allocation of advertisers' spending that ensued, had transformed the mediascape in ways that needed to be addressed in regulatory terms. With regard to commercial communications, there was a "grey area" (Reding 2006: 6) that had been awaiting clarification, and that was the legal status of product placement. The TVWF Directive did not specifically forbid nor allow this practice, but the prevailing legal interpretation across member states (including Italy) was to treat product placement as a form of surreptitious advertising, which was prohibited by Article 10 Point 4 of the directive. At the same time, though, the practice of placing branded products in films had been "unofficially" used (and tolerated) in Italy and elsewhere for decades (see Chapter 1).

At the EU level, the debate over the opportunity to legalise product placement in films and television programmes was a heated one. Stakeholders divided into two main positions. Some, including the BBC and the European Federation of Journalists, opposed the legalisation of product placement in its entirety. Others supported the legalisation of product placement, but with restrictions on product categories, on the genres of programmes allowed, and advocated the provision of clear identification measures. This latter position was held, for example, by the European Broadcasting Union, the Association of Commercial Television in Europe, and also by the World Federation of Advertisers (Ginosar 2012). In Italy, there was a general consensus among advertisers and audiovisual operators in favour of a (limited) legalisation of product placement. Film producers welcomed the practice as a way to increase budget sources in a time of public funding cuts (ANICA 2008). National broadcasters RAI and Mediaset, both of which had their own branches in film production (RAI Cinema and Medusa respectively) and advertising sales (SIPRA and Publitalia), welcomed deregulation as an opportunity for expanding their businesses. Also in favour of deregulation were Italian advertisers who saw product placement as a desirable innovation in an otherwise stale market (Ranalli 2008). Even the Italian communications' regulatory authority, AGCOM, wished for product placement to reach the "largest possible expansion" (Ranalli 2008).

The debate over allowing product placement in audiovisual media saw one overarching and recurring argument advanced by both sides: the comparison with the US. Those against the legalisation feared an excessive commercialisation of European cinema and television, whose roots, unlike the US, were strongly grounded in arthouse productions and public service broadcasting. On the other hand, those in favour of the legalisation called for the necessity of creating a level playing field with the already

The imperfect marketisation 67

powerful Hollywood competitors, who had always made extensive (and essentially unregulated) use of product placement. This latter argument, in particular, was advanced by the European Commission in the person of the then Commissioner for Information Society and Media Viviane Reding. In a speech held in front of representatives of the Swiss press, Reding stated:

> For some years, we have been faced in the European media industry with a phenomenon we have known for quite some time from American films, which is not covered at all by existing legislation, namely product placement. (…) But let's be serious: product placement is a reality. (…) The unclear legal situation and different laws in Europe not only deceive the consumer but put the European film makers at a big disadvantage compared to their US competitors.
>
> (Reding 2006: 5–6)

As we shall see shortly, referencing the US as the model market for product placement is something that Italian marketing and film practitioners do quite often, generally to point out deficiencies within their domestic system. The debate in the EU over the legalisation of product placement went on for over four years, between 2003, when the commission launched a public consultation on the matter, and 2007, when the new 2007/65/EC Audiovisual Media Services Without Frontiers Directive was issued. The latter was subsequently codified, i.e. incorporated, into Directive 2010/13/EU, known as Audiovisual Media Services (AVMS). The conflicting positions expressed by representatives of the member states, and institutional and industrial actors emerge from the complex and at times counter-intuitive wording of the final text of the directive. The directive states that, as a general rule, "product placement shall be prohibited", but, immediately after, it goes on to say that "by way of derogation (…) product placement shall be admissible" under certain circumstances (Article 11). Such an unusual and potentially confusing phrasing was eventually abandoned in the latest version of the directive, which entered into force in December 2018. EU Directive 2018/1808, which will need to be transposed into national legislations by September 2020, is more straightforward in stating, "Product placement *shall be allowed* in all audiovisual media services, except in news and current affairs programmes, consumer affairs programmes, religious programmes and children's programmes" (Article 11).[1] The general provisions regarding product categories and modes of placement have remained essentially unchanged: product placement is forbidden for tobacco (including e-cigarettes) and prescription medicines;[2] it shall not give undue prominence to the product; and viewers shall be clearly informed about its presence in films and television shows, as well as (and

68 *The imperfect marketisation*

this a new addition) audiovisual content available on video-sharing Internet platforms (Article 11, Directive 2018/1808/EU). However, by reversing the general prohibition on product placement, the European Commission has demonstrated a clear change of pace in the traditionally cautious opening towards commercial communications in EU audiovisual contents.

The points of contention that emerged during the debate for the legalisation of product placement in the EU mostly concerned television content. This was originally due to the airwaves' spectrum scarcity as well as to the prominent role that television continues to play as a public sphere institution (Cushion 2012). However, EU-made films intended for theatrical release were also subject to the same restrictions concerning product categories, undue prominence, and identification. Unlike television, though, where the presence of product placement needs to be disclosed at the start, at the end of the programme, and after each advertising break, in motion pictures paid-for inclusion of products and brands should simply be announced in the closing titles. This is the same rule that Italian policymakers established when they first legalised product placement in cinema three years earlier than the first European directive on the subject.

Lights, camera, brands!

Between 2004 and 2010, Italian governments issued a series of policies aimed at reforming the overall system of funding for national film production, and for the film industry more generally. Some of these reforms were enacted during the centre-right legislatures led by Silvio Berlusconi (2001–2006, 2008–2011), whilst others under the centre-left coalition of Romano Prodi (2006–2008). The former of such reforms was the legalisation of product placement, and it was introduced in 2004 by the so-called Urbani decree from the then Minister of Cultural Heritage and Activities (D. Lgs. 22 January 2004, n. 28). The latter of these reform laws was the introduction of tax incentives for companies investing in national film production (Law 24 December 2007, n. 244; and Ministerial Decree 21 January 2010), and it will be discussed in the next section. Both the product placement and the tax incentive policies were driven by a common goal to open the Italian film production market to economic actors whose core business lay outside the audiovisual sector. Economic savings was a major reason for that and so was the will to rationalise the distribution of public funding, which, until then, had brought poor returns, both in terms of the producers' ability to repay the funds and of the funded films to have a significant cultural impact (Cucco and Manzoli 2017). The 2004 Urbani decree established a new "reference system", which essentially included a series of points that the submitted projects would score on the basis of measures such as box office results

The imperfect marketisation 69

of previous films made by the production company, number and quality of awards previously received, the curriculum of the prospective cast, and so on. In this sense, the reform gave priority to the entrepreneurial reliability of the production company over the quality of the screenplay submitted. The legalisation of product placement stems from the same rationale: to allow for a more diverse, hence financially sustainable, set of economic sources to be accessible by film producers, beyond direct state funding.

The Italian Ministry of Cultural Heritage and Activities saw product placement as a new and potentially powerful promotional vehicle for *Made in Italy* merchandise, which, that same year, received clearer and stricter legal protection by means of a dedicated rule on the use of *Made in Italy* labelling (Law 24 December 2003, n. 350, Article 4, Point 49). This was the position of Gaetano Blandini, then director-general of the ministry's cinema section:

> [Product placement] is not the panacea for all the evils of our cinema, nor, in particular, for the whole economic and financial crisis that has gone through it for a certain period. There is no doubt, however, that this is an opportunity to be used and exploited in the best possible way, convincing even our auteurs that product placement in no way diminishes the artistic quality of their projects and products. (...) Rather, it is a question of giving it the right place, especially within Italian films, to the Made-in-Italy, to the national product.
>
> (ANICA 2008: 9, my translation from original Italian)

Made in Italy products had been integrated in foreign films well before its legalisation by national laws, and the trend has continued in the 2000s. We already mentioned the exemplary case of Vespa, but many other Italian brands had been enjoying international visibility, notably through Hollywood films. From Richard Gere's all-Armani wardrobe in *American Gigolo* (dir. Schrader 1980) to the San Pellegrino bottle poured for Meryl Streep/Miranda Priestly in *The Devil Wears Prada* (dir. Frankel 2006); from Matt Damon cooking Garofalo pasta in *Hereafter* (dir. Eastwood 2011) to the overindulgence of brands in Woody Allen's *To Rome with Love* (2012) (Peroni beer, Illy coffee, Beretta cured meats, FIAT cars, etc.) to Ryan Gosling's apartment in *La La Land* (dir. Chazelle 2016), equipped with SMEG design appliances. During the first eight years after its legalisation in Italy, companies operating in the traditional sectors of *Made in Italy* started to also place their products in domestic films, with a majority of occurrences from fashion and jewellery brands (39.5 per cent); tourism and travel (11.8 per cent); motors (11.3 per cent); luxury brands (5.2 per cent); and food and beverages (4.5 per cent) (Nelli 2013: 260). With regard to

70 *The imperfect marketisation*

the film genres mostly concerned by product placement, comedies strongly prevailed (77.1 per cent) over dramas (17.5 per cent) and other genres (5.2 per cent) (Nelli 2013: 233).

Tax credits: The Italian way

The second, major policy change introduced by the Italian government to attract private capital into the film production market was the provision of tax incentives for non-audiovisual companies. Before the 2008 Budget Law (Law 24 December 2007), the Italian state did not provide any form of tax incentives for companies operating or investing in national cinema. This constituted a shortcoming, especially considering that virtually all other European countries already had such measures in place (Olsberg and Barnes 2014). At the international level, tax incentives for the film industry comprise three main types of schemes: cash rebates, i.e. the reimbursement of a fixed quota of the expenses incurred by a production company; tax shelter; and tax credit. Tax shelter, which provides a company with economic savings by reducing its taxable income, was initially introduced by the Italian government. This proved ineffective and was eventually repealed, as the majority of Italian film companies, whose business traditionally relied for a significant part on state funding, did not produce large taxable incomes (Olsberg and Barnes 2014). Tax credit, instead, proved more successful, as it reduced a company's due taxes on the basis of a fixed percentage set by the law. Law No. 244 introduced tax credit for every category of companies operating in the film industry: producers, distributors, exhibitors, post-production, and technical services. Moreover, the law opened this measure also to external, i.e. non-audiovisual companies, that invested in national film production. The tax credit was originally set to 40 per cent of the external company's investment (D. M. 21 January 2010), then reduced to 30 per cent (D. M. 15 March 2018), up to a maximum of one million euros per year.

The tax credit was itself a form of indirect public funding, but one that weighed considerably less on the state's coffers compared to the direct funding that the (shrinking) FUS provided. Indeed, as Figure 3.1 shows, as the various forms of tax credit became operative (the ministry's implementation decrees were issued between 2009 and 2011), the balance between direct and indirect state funding shifted in favour of this latter. This actually contrasts to other EU countries, where the introduction of tax incentives did not coincide with a reduction in direct funding for the film sector (Olsberg and Barnes 2014).

Figure 3.1 also shows the growing financial importance within Italian cinema of external companies, whose investments now account for an average of nearly 15 per cent of the total budget of an Italian film (ANICA 2017: 5).

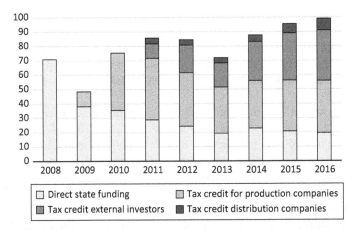

Figure 3.1 State funding to national film production: direct vs. indirect funding. (From ANICA, 2017, "Tutti i numeri del cinema italiano - anno 2017", www.anica.it/documentazione-e-dati-annuali-2/tutti-i-numeri-del-cinema-italiano-anno-2017.)

Under the tax credit policy, non-audiovisual and film production companies form a joint venture (*associazione in partecipazione*), whereby the external investor shares both in the film's profits and in the possible losses, up to a maximum of 70 per cent of the total earnings (Article 26, D. M. 15 March 2018). What's particularly interesting for the issue at stake here is that the law allowed non-audiovisual companies to combine tax credit and product placement-related investment in one film. Thus, one company can invest in the same film for the twofold purpose of financial and promotional return, provided that its investment covers at least 5 per cent of the overall film production budget (Article 2, Point 4, D. M. 21 January 2010). The opportunity to combine tax credit and product placement–related investments, which policymakers introduced in 2010, was crucial in stimulating external companies into getting involved in Italian film production.

3.4 The Italian market for brands and films

The 2004 legalisation of product placement and the introduction of tax incentives for external companies brought important changes to the Italian film and marketing industries. The opportunities created by the law for brands and films to collaborate required the development of new skill sets and expertise. Film producers' and advertisers' professional cultures

72   *The imperfect marketisation*

changed as they learned to adapt, and in some cases to assume the language, the identities, and the mentality of their new partners, as we shall see in the remainder of the chapter.[3] From an industrial and organisational standpoint, the legalisation of product placement and external tax credit led, in some cases, to the creation of new businesses and dedicated professional figures, and, in others, to a reorganisation of tasks and roles within pre-existing groups.

The Italian market for brands and films comprises three main actors: the advertisers, the film producers, and the promotional intermediaries. In Italy, promotional intermediaries play an essential role not only in mediating the complex nexus between artistic production and commercial communication, but also in training advertisers and film producers for a relatively new market. In the case of product placement, for example, only a minority of deals are directly handled by representatives of the film production and the consumer company. Only one Italian production company has internalised the product placement–related activities and that is Filmauro, the parent company of the *cinepanettoni* (see previous section *Italy to drink* in Chapter 2). The majority of agreements are initiated, managed, and finalised via promotional intermediaries (Nelli and Patruno 2014), and yet, their work remains little known to the general audience. Viewers are thus mostly unaware of how significant the work of such intermediaries may be in shaping the films and audiovisual content they consume. The remainder of this chapter will shed light on the practices and cultures surrounding product placement, external tax credit, and branded entertainment initiatives between Italian film producers and advertisers by presenting the voices of the practitioners involved, with special attention devoted to the key role played by promotional intermediaries.

"It's all an intermediation"

A remarkable aspect to be noted about Italian promotional intermediaries working with advertisers and film producers for activities such as product placement, external tax credit, and co-marketing is that they define themselves as *entertainment marketing companies*, rather than *advertising agencies*. Here is how one of my interviewees explained this choice to me:

> Ours is not an advertising *agency*, we don't call ourselves an *agency*: this is an *entertainment marketing company*. The *agency* has an advertising notion to it, whereas us, knowing so well cinema and all the implications and challenges of the film industry, we work for the production companies to help them find financing, and for consumer companies to help them communicate in the best way possible. (PI 1)[4]

The imperfect marketisation   73

We will address this lexicon usage (made by promotional intermediaries, but not by film producers) in further detail over the final chapter of the book. For now, it is important to note that the fact that Italian promotional intermediaries distinguish themselves, also semantically, from advertising agencies derives from the desire to (self-)represent themselves as a new and specific professional category, as well as to signal a difference in the corporate structure and ownership profile of their companies versus those of "traditional" Italian ad agencies. Unlike the majority of traditional advertising agencies, entertainment marketing companies are not owned by the holding companies that dominate the global advertising market, i.e. WPP, Omnicom, Publicis, and Interpublic. They are a handful of companies mostly based in Milan, the national advertising hub, and Rome, the capital of Italian cinema. Among these, the ones that provided me with access and with the opportunity to conduct interviews were Camelot, QMI, and Pch Media. Most of these companies were established around 2004 to seize the new business opportunities introduced by the legalisation of product placement. Others pre-existed as marketing companies and, since 2004, incorporated product placement among their services. Few of these companies were founded in 2010, following the legalisation of external tax credit, which they included in their service offer for film producers and distributors, along with product placement and co-marketing activities. Instead, some of them operate, through non-exclusive deals, as local agents for Hollywood majors, to plan and implement promotional activities for the Italian market or to provide *Made in Italy* products to be placed in US movies. The dynamics in place between Hollywood studios and Italian entertainment marketing companies for these types of activities are those typical of "network capitalism", where relatively autonomous globally distributed firm units cooperate to maximise profits and achieve competitive advantages, under the centralised control of a corporation (Fuchs 2003).

The business model of Italian entertainment marketing companies varies according to the type of operation they are to run. In the case of the external tax credit, these companies act as agents for film producers, who hire them to search for companies interested in investing in their productions. When they are called to design and implement marketing activities, they are put under contract by the party that commissions the operation, which can be either an advertiser or a film distribution company. In all these cases, the entertainment marketing company works exclusively for a single client, even if the operation requires it to initiate and manage a partnership with a third party. Conversely, when it comes to product placement things get muddier, as the intermediation that these companies provide is remunerated by both sides involved in the deal. Product placement collaborations are initiated by film producers, who provide them with scripts of their upcoming

74   *The imperfect marketisation*

film productions. Intermediaries scan the scripts for possible scenes and dialogues in which to insert products or brand references, and then proceed to search for relevant advertisers. Effectively, when seeking possible brand partners, promotional intermediaries also provide a service to advertisers, for whom they create new opportunities for commercial communication. Indeed, in the case of product placement deals, intermediaries receive a fee from the film producer (generally around 20 per cent of the advertiser's investment in the film) *as well as* a fee from the advertiser that places its product(s) in the film. Such a business model differs from the one generally adopted by promotional intermediaries in the US, which, as previously noted, is the benchmark Italian operators reportedly aspire to.

> How it works in the US is that you get paid by the advertiser. And on the other hand, nothing. You deal with the producer on behalf of your client. In Italy everything is much greyer, and, in my opinion, it doesn't work so well because, since it's all a negotiation, it's all an intermediation, it would be fairer to understand whom you're negotiating for. (PI 2)

This *modus operandi* produces a situation of poor transparency in the product placement market, which resembles that of the Italian television advertising market, where price lists for commercial breaks, whilst officially present, are in fact purely indicative and subject to fluctuations of up to 90 per cent (Pitteri 2006). Italian promotional intermediaries, whilst acknowledging this structural anomaly in the market, are reluctant to recognise their own role in perpetuating such an anomaly:

> If we are conducting a communication campaign for the client, the client pays us like a regular agency. On the other side, it may be that we are also paid by the film producer or distributor. It's not really something we like to talk about. Because it's kind of, say, our own business. (PI 2)

Once the product placement deal is finalised, a representative of the entertainment marketing company follows its implementation during the critical phase of film shooting. Promotional intermediaries admit that their being on set is quite disliked by Italian filmmakers, but their presence is a guarantee for the sponsor:

> For the filmmaker, the most important thing is the artistic output, while the advertiser asks for figures and measurable results. In all of this, the function of the agency is very sensitive, it is a matter of putting in communication two very different worlds which sometimes are at odds with each other. (PI 3)

The imperfect marketisation 75

Thus, with their presence on and off set, promotional intermediaries fulfil a function that can be considered one of "language" mediation and process facilitation between two otherwise foreign professional cultures.

Film producers get organised

Italian film production companies are characterised by a relatively low degree of labour segmentation, especially when compared to the organisational structures of Hollywood studios (Miller et al. 2004). When it comes to the collaborative relationships with external companies, Italian film production companies organise themselves according to four main models.[5] Some production companies have a professional figure dedicated to managing both product placement and tax credit agreements. This is especially the case for companies working with bigger budgets, often for international co-productions. In other cases, product placement and external tax credit deals are entrusted to two separate figures within the executive production department: the former with a commercial background and the latter with a stronger financial profile. In the third organisational model, the producer personally manages the external tax credit, but delegates product placement to another person within the production department. This latter model derives from the fact that the tax credit generally allows for more conspicuous funds to be raised, compared to product placement alone, hence the producer's will to follow this type of deal more closely. Finally, in small-scale film companies, the producer takes on the task of managing both product placement and tax credit investments. In this latter case, things are more complicated for promotional intermediaries, who find themselves interacting with someone who has to juggle all the main production-related aspects. The company's size is the single most important factor to determine the organisational management of product placement and tax credit within Italian film production companies; annual frequency and economic scope of the agreements, though, also play a role.

As regards the relationship with the promotional intermediaries, film production companies show a dual attitude towards them. One producer, from a leading Rome-based production company, told me that dealing with a promotional intermediary, as opposed to the advertiser itself, may make the collaboration process slower.

> Not having an agency that acts as your intermediary, we have often noticed that you can close things quickly. Because we make a request to the company, maybe we sit around a table, we propose two or three things directly, and instead maybe the agency, by its very nature, takes slower steps because every time it has to report to the client. (FP 1)

76   *The imperfect marketisation*

That same producer, though, admits that entertainment marketing companies may create new partnership opportunities, which would not be available to film producers via direct contacts.

> For me it is important to have both direct and mediated contacts with advertisers. The agency can put you in contact with clients you don't know. For example, we did product placements with S. Pellegrino, that we had no prior contact with; we did placements with Nestlé, Lavazza, which didn't come from our own contacts. So, absolutely, intermediation companies do work, but they make the relationship a multipart one. (FP 1)

For Italian film producers, working with intermediaries has its main benefits in the larger pool of advertisers' contacts these can access; in the consultancy work that intermediaries do to facilitate the mutual understanding between partners from different business areas (although this also means potentially longer and multiparty negotiations); and in the intermediaries' ability to keep the collaboration with external investors in place even when the work schedules of the two partners do not match. In this regard, the product placement manager of a film production company said:

> From production to post-production, a film can take as long as one year, from the first drafting of the screenplay, to the film's release. So, on the one hand, the time is quite slow, but on the other hand, when the cast is established and the project is finalised, within a few weeks we start. So, there is a phase in which external companies must necessarily decide whether or not to join the project, because, after that, technically, there is no longer time to join in. (FP 2)

Whilst this is always the case for tax credit, which requires, by law, the establishment of a joint venture between film and external companies; in the case of product placement, latecomers may still have the chance to place their brands in the scenes of a film, thanks to the digital technologies used in the post-production phase. Digital technology may also be used to rework a product placement that, because of a film's prolonged working timescale, has meanwhile become obsolete. The opportunities provided by digital technologies of making brand insertions more flexible and potentially viable also retrospectively have important consequences on a film's shooting phase. We will address this point in the remainder of this chapter, which deals with the concrete effects that product placement and tax credit agreements have on all the major steps of cinematic production.

3.5 Who serves whom? The creative impact of brands in films

The collaborations between film companies and external investors—whether for product placement, tax credit, or branded entertainment purposes—have different consequences on the film production process and outcome, depending on two main factors: firstly, at what stage of the production progress the agreement with the external partner is finalised, and secondly, the amount of the partner's investment in relation to the overall film budget. These two factors are mostly interconnected. As a general rule, the sooner the collaboration agreement is finalised, the greater is the opportunity for the external company to exert leverage on key aspects of a film's creative development and production. Likewise, early secured investments are generally larger, which also means a greater power to steer the production outcome. For such reasons, promotional intermediaries tend to push film producers and advertisers to collaborate from the earlier phase of the screenwriting process. This enables screenwriters to design situations, settings, and dialogues that integrate the investor's product and brand values more effectively, while also allowing producers to negotiate more conspicuous budgets, both in the form of real money investments and in media value. On the other side, when a brand decides to commit to a film project from its early stages, it is generally in a stronger position to negotiate greater visibility for its brand in the film and in the film's promotional paratexts, but also to have access to exclusive visual material, such as film stills, quotes, and graphics, that can be used as branded content in the external company's media outlets. The opportunity to leverage a product placement or a tax credit operation to create a larger, trans-media branded content operation is increasingly important for investors. Indeed, branded content is becoming the currency with which advertisers estimate the value of a product placement or a tax credit operation, as this promotional intermediary explained:

> On the Internet you need content to communicate. These operations [product placement and tax credit] generate content. I mean, typically the product placement contracts used to be "How many scenes [is my product into]? How many seconds? How is it visible?" Now it is about "How many backstage videos do you give me? How many images from the set?" Because the company then use them online, on social media, so what we negotiate with the distributor has changed. That is, I [as investor] am not that interested in how much you [as film company] show of me in the film; I'm more interested in what you give me as ammunition for the web. (PI 2)

On the other side of the negotiation, the media value brought by advertisers to film producers and distributors is touted by promotional intermediaries.

78 *The imperfect marketisation*

In referencing the case of *Il ricco, il povero e il maggiordomo* ("The rich, the poor and the butler") (dir. Bertacca, 2014), starring popular Italian TV–born comedy trio Aldo, Giovanni & Giacomo, an executive from an entertainment marketing company explained to me:

> What did the consumer company bring to the film? They brought money, via a product placement deal. They brought media value to advertise the film: they did a teaser campaign six months prior to the release, where they announced that an Aldo, Giovanni and Giacomo film was coming soon, and they did so in their stores. Finally, the consumer company contributed to the film's box office, by giving away tickets to their customers. (PI 2)

For film producers, though, the media value brought by advertisers is not necessarily as straightforward: "The marketing activities mostly serves *them*," a film producer said, referring to external investors. Moreover, the same producer expressed concern about external companies making (or trying to make) unfair uses of film stills in their media outlets: "For example, say we negotiated for an actor's picture to be used only in an internal newsletter, and still *they* use it online, pretending that is a newsletter. We've been burned many times" (FP 1). The way this film producer uses a "we/they" discourse here speaks of a much more contentious scenario for branded content operations than the smooth win–win situation described earlier by the promotional intermediary.

As regards the amount of the investments made by external companies, while product placement alone does not usually top 5 per cent of a film's production budget, when it is coupled with tax credit and/or co-marketing operations, the combined value can go up to 30 per cent. Indeed, the multiple returns (financial, fiscal, and promotional) that the external company can receive from the joint use of tax credit, product placement, and co-marketing activities justify higher spending and reduce economic risks. This produces a somewhat paradoxical situation whereby measures like tax credit and co-marketing that, by their nature, have no direct impact on a film's look and narrative features, when combined with product placement, become powerful ways for external companies to influence the film's creative output. How such influence may concretely play out and how do Italian filmmakers and producers manage it will be at the centre of the upcoming sections.

"They made up an ad hoc *scene"*

The script is the starting point for planning and implementing the presence of a brand or a product into a film. This presence can be either in the form of a visual appearance and/or an aural reference to the sponsor, most

The imperfect marketisation   79

often done through a verbal mention in the dialogues. As the promotional intermediary scans the script for ways to include the sponsor, three main scenarios may emerge: the script offers the opportunity to place the sponsor with no changes needed; the script offers opportunities for placement, with only minor adjustments needed; the script, as it is, presents no opportunities for placement, so major changes are required to integrate the sponsor's brand or product. The former case is what one of the Italian promotional intermediaries I interviewed defined (using the English language) a "lucky opportunity" (PI 1). This was the case, for example, of the product placement of COOP branded coffee in the comedy *Il comandante e la cicogna* (*The Commander and the Stork*) (dir. Soldini, 2012). In the film, characterised by a surreal tone, the deceased wife of the protagonist makes recurring returns as a ghost. In her appearances, the ghost allows herself some small pleasures that she lost along with her earthly life. Her favourite one is to take the coffee jar from the kitchen cupboard and smell the aroma, of which she is very nostalgic. The coffee jar skit was in the original script, but the agreement with Italian company COOP put a specific brand on the product.

In the second case scenario, when minor adjustments are required, it is the promotional intermediary, in agreement with the film's production department, that makes the change. As a product placement manager told me:

> If the script reads "The girl takes a bottle of beer out of the fridge" and you have a product placement with a ready pasta product, you just change it into "The girl takes the ready pasta out of the fridge", without disturbing the screenwriter, you just make the replacement and that's fine. (FP 2)

In such cases, the production department is responsible for ensuring that the beer bottle originally included in the script does not bear particular relevance for the story or the characterisation, so that the placement of the ready pasta sponsor does not collide with the filmmaker's artistic vision.

The third case scenario is the most critical one. When the original script does not offer suitable opportunities, the production needs to ask the screenwriters to design new ways to integrate the sponsor's product. This may entail writing a scene from scratch, as screenwriters have done for the placement of Di Saronno liqueur in *The Commander and the Stork*: "In the script there was nothing like that, there was nothing about alcohol, so we had to ask the screenwriters 'How do we place this?' They made up an *ad hoc* scene" (FP 2). This may also entail writing new dialogue and creating new expedients inside an existing scene. In the comedy *Benvenuto Presidente!* (*Welcome Mr. President!*) (dir. Milani, 2013) a quiet man living in a small mountain village is suddenly and unexpectedly catapulted to the

80 *The imperfect marketisation*

top of Italian political institutions. Early on in the film, a scene shows us the protagonist that, whilst enjoying a cookout with friends, is scolded by his careerist son for not being ambitious enough, as, in the current economic climate, the son says, "everyone is fighting to take the bread out of the competitors' mouth." To these words, the protagonist (played by TV comedian Claudio Bisio) gestures towards the farm's entrance, saying: "Bread? Do you want bread? Here's the bread! Morato, bring out the bread!" An elderly, smiling man walks out the door with two large loaves of packaged sliced bread in his hands, to the cheers of the guests: it's Luigi Morato himself, founder and CEO of the homonymous bread company. Whilst the cookout scene was originally in the script, Morato's entrance and the mention of his brand were introduced upon the company's explicit request, as the film producer explained:

> Morato's people came and said, "Yes, it's a good movie, but there must be Mr. Morato in the scene. We must have Mr. Morato in a scene." (…) So, I accompanied the gentlemen to the door and banged my head against the wall. Then I remembered that there was a scene in the film in which Bisio was cooking, right there, on the spot. (…) I begged the director and Bisio to insert a scene in which Bisio, who was at the barbecue, said something like "Speaking of bread, Morato, have you brought bread?" And Mr. Morato would come out with these loaves of bread. (FP 3)

In trying to convince the creative crew to accept such a prominent and unusual placement, the producer referenced the company's conspicuous investment, both in the form of tax credit and product placement: "I said to them 'Please, let's do this!' Because, first, this way the film gets done, and, second, thankfully Mr. Morato and his brand are not that popular, it could still be done. So, we managed to do this scene" (FP 3).

There can also be a case where the investment of an external company determines a change in the film's shooting location, as one promotional intermediary told me:

> There's this one film, *Scusate se esisto* ("Sorry if I exist") in which Focchi, a company specialised in industrial curtain walls has made an external tax credit and a product placement operation, and they even succeeded in having some scenes shot in London, thus moving the entire crew to London, where they had an active construction site. (PI 4)

In these latter cases, the external companies' ability to provoke significant changes in the film's original script (even to the despair of the producers—"I

The imperfect marketisation   81

banged my head against the wall") derived from the amount of their investments, not only in product placement, but also in tax credit. The latter, by effectively making the external investor a co-producer of the film, gives them greater strength and legitimacy vis-à-vis the production as well as the creative cast, as all the Italian promotional intermediaries I interviewed have confirmed.

"We pay more attention to the logo"

The creative impact that the collaborations with advertisers and tax credit investors exert on the film production process cascades from the screenwriting phase down to the shooting phase. This is true regardless of whether the placements require a specific intervention from the screenwriter. In terms of camera movements, type and length of the shots, and lighting of the scene, product placement requires special attention on the part of the film crew, as the product placement manager of an Italian production company explained:

> If there's a van in the scene, whether it's FIAT or another brand, some van has to be there, so we use a van. (...) In short, for me [as part of the film production] it's not so much about having to use certain products, as it is about how these products have to be seen. We could use the product the same way [also without a commercial agreement], but with a placement we give the product more prominence, we pay more attention to the logo, to the product's functionality, things we wouldn't do without an agreement in place. (FP 2)

The producer informs all departments of the existence of a commercial agreement and these departments must adapt their work to what the placement requires. For example, if the sponsor's product is part of the set dressing or decoration, the art department must ensure that the product in question is used and given the right visibility. At the same time, it must also make sure that it does not give accidental visibility to products of competing brands. For their part, the camera and lighting department, as well as the director and assistant directors, must ensure that the sponsor's product is illuminated, framed and, if need be, handled by the performers in a manner consistent with what had been agreed with the advertiser.

Actors and actresses are essential for ensuring the implementation of a product placement operation. Even the slightest deviation from what has been written (and agreed upon) in the script can undo months of negotiations. In this regard, one of my interviewees, who worked for the industry body representing Italian advertisers (UPA), reported an example from *This Must Be the Place* (dir. Sorrentino, 2011), an Italian, French, and Irish co-production starring Sean Penn as a depressed middle-aged former rock star,

82 *The imperfect marketisation*

and Frances McDormand as his beloved wife. In one of the early sequences, we see the protagonist browsing through supermarket aisles, stopping in front of the frozen food section and, after careful consideration, putting into his cart a Valsoia-branded frozen pizza. In the following scene, the pizza is being cooked in the kitchen oven and, to his wife asking, "What's for dinner?" the protagonist replies: "Veggie pizza". This latter line, though, was not the one that Valsoia and the film production company, both Italian, had agreed upon. Instead, Sean Penn's character should have reportedly said "Vegan pizza", as Valsoia's brand identity and selling point rely precisely in its being a vegan-only food company. Such a minor script change, whilst unimportant for the film's narrative flow or characterisation, has the potential to undermine in significant ways the advertiser's message, hence the overall value of the placement operation on their part.[6]

Finally, it is interesting to note that product placement has the potential to affect the shooting of a film even when it is not there (yet). Speaking about the production of the romantic comedy *Io e lei* (*Me, Myself and Her*) (dir. Tognazzi, 2015), the film's producer explained to me how the director and her crew organised the shooting so as to leave an option open for the insertion of a brand even after the phase of work on the set was over.

> In the film we have a scene in which the two [*female*] protagonists are in front their bathroom's mirror, putting creams on their faces before going to bed: to us, it looked like a great opportunity to make a nice product placement. We tried to contact consumer companies beforehand and they weren't interested, so what did we do? We shot the scene in two ways. (…) We shot one version of the scene with a cream chosen by the director, and then we shot another one with an unbranded container. We did so with the idea of inserting the detail of the brand in post-production, in the event of… (FP 2)

As previously mentioned, digital technology allows for the opportunity to insert or modify a product placement well after the film has been shot. In this latter case, the mere possibility of a product placement exerted a significant influence on the film production, especially if we consider that each additional take significantly prolongs, and thus increases the cost of, shooting the film.

The final cut

For a company that places its brand or product within a film, the phase of the production process that presents the greatest pitfalls is the editing phase. One reason for that is that, as a general rule, no member of the production

The imperfect marketisation   83

department is present throughout the editing work. During the shooting phase, the product placement manager (or any other relevant production figure) monitors that the product is shown or used in accordance with the terms agreed with the advertiser, and, if not, they can intervene on the spot or discuss the change with the advertiser. However, the advertiser has no way of applying such control within the editing room, where only the film's editor and director are generally present. From a creative perspective, the editing phase is the trickiest for the advertiser because product placement contracts usually provide that the film's final cut, including the scenes where the sponsor is present, is the sole responsibility of the director and the production. This does not mean that the advertiser has no agency in determining how the presence of its product is edited into the film: the Morato product placement scene mentioned in the previous section is a striking example of such agency. However, it does mean that the director retains the right to the final, decisive creative act of the film production process, i.e. the editing. Such a clause could easily discourage advertisers from investing in a film. For this reason, production companies, in agreement with the promotional intermediaries, provide for instalment payments for placement operations: one instalment at the time of signing the contract, the second at the end of the editing phase, and the third after the film's theatrical release. In some cases, production companies may also accept a single payment once the shooting is complete (PI 2, PI 3).

Despite the efforts made by the film producer and the promotional intermediary to keep creative and commercial aspects together, sometimes the wishes of the advertiser and the director's right to final cut are irreparably incompatible. A telling illustration of such dynamics is provided by the failed product placement operation of Di Saronno in the Academy Award-winning film *La Grande Bellezza* (*The Great Beauty*) (dir. Sorrentino, 2013). To this regard, the film producer admitted having returned the money that Di Saronno had paid for appearing in the film, as the shot with the brand's characteristic squared-shape bottle was cut out from the final version of the editing (FP 3). Even worse, from the advertiser's perspective, was the fact that the film gave major prominence to a competing brand: Martini. Indeed, *The Great Beauty* opens to a sequence (likely the most memorable of the whole film) set on the rooftop of a Roman building where the crowded, loud, and kitsch birthday party of the protagonist, played by renowned actor Toni Servillo, is in full swing. The scene is dominated by the large, real-life Martini neon sign, located on top of a building near Rome's central via Veneto. That sign was not the result of a commercial agreement with the manufacturer, but an essential part of the message and aesthetic feeling that the film aimed to convey, as one of the film's producers told me: "The director wanted to keep Martini at all costs

84   *The imperfect marketisation*

because, to him, it was a very important visual reference: via Veneto, *La Dolce Vita...*" (FP 2).[7]

In the case of *The Great Beauty*, the presence of a celebrated auteur, Paolo Sorrentino, and leading actor, Toni Servillo, has proved both an advantage and a hurdle for the actualisation of branded operations inside and around the film, as a promotional intermediary told me:

> With Sorrentino's film it was easy to attract interest from advertisers; it was very difficult to finalise it, because, between Toni Servillo and Paolo Sorrentino, it was impossible to meet the needs of the external companies which, by putting money in the film, they want their needs to be met. (PI 1)

The creative control that a film production company is able to retain over how product placement operations are implemented is certainly higher when the film's artistic cast has a higher status. This has to do with the power that auteur theory traditionally entrusts to the director as the ultimate holder of a film project. Such power, especially in the case of the Italian film industry, well surpasses that of the film producer (Nicoli 2017). Consequently, film producers tend to push more for the advertiser's need to be satisfied when the film is less artistically ambitious, rather than when it is more commercial and middlebrow. This has clearly emerged in the different attitudes shown by the very same producers in the case of a more popular comedy, like *Benvenuto Presidente* (*Welcome Mr. President*), as opposed to a more arthouse production, like *La Grande Bellezza* (*The Great Beauty*).

Notes

1 Whether the UK will need to implement the new Audiovisual Media Services Directive will depend on the terms that will be agreed with the EU with regard to Brexit (deal or no-deal scenario). At the time of writing (April 2019) the transition period of Brexit has been extended until the end of 2020, so, if things do not change in the meantime, the UK shall transpose the provisions of Directive 2018/1808 into binding national law. However, if a no-deal scenario occurs, EU directives will no longer automatically apply to the UK, which will have to decide whether to retain or amend existing EU laws.

2 Member states had the opportunity to opt out entirely from the practice—as Denmark did, after an initial authorisation in 2013 (Sandfeld Jakobsen 2013)— or to set additional restrictions, particularly on product categories. The UK, for instance, extended the ban to all alcoholic drinks; foods or drinks high in fat, salt, or sugar; gambling services; infant formula; and all medicinal products (Ofcom 2019). In Italy, the provisions set by the EU were incorporated in the single text of the laws on radio and television (*Testo unico sulla radiotelevisione*, D. Lgs. 31 July 2005, n. 177) without any alteration from the original provisions.

The imperfect marketisation 85

3 For more comprehensive accounts on the co-mingling of advertisers' and film and television producers' professional culture in the Anglo-American context, see Caldwell (2008), Davis (2013), and Grainge and Johnson (2015).
4 For confidentiality reasons, I will not provide the names of the practitioners I interviewed. Instead, I will reference promotional intermediaries and film producers with the letters PI and FP, respectively, followed by numbers in ascending order.
5 The Italian film production companies I was able to access to conduct interviews with producers and product placement managers are Indigo Film and Lumière Film. Additional data and information were retrieved through interface ethnography (Ortner 2009) at film and marketing trade events with the film production companies Cattleya, Indiana Production, and Italian International Film.
6 My interviewee at UPA could not confirm nor deny whether this change in the dialogue led the advertiser to renegotiate the agreement with the production company. However, this seems unlikely, given Sean Penn's international status, which anyway confers prestige to Valsoia's promotional operation.
7 In 2017, Paolo Sorrentino went on to direct a piece of branded entertainment for one of Martini's competing brand, Campari. The short video, titled *Killer in Red* and starring American actor Clive Owen as a mysterious bartender, places Sorrentino among other prestigious artists who, throughout the 20th century, created advertising for the Campari brand: among them, Fortunato Depero and Federico Fellini (see Chapter 1, section "Advertising modernity").

4 Conclusions

The previous chapters have endeavoured to paint an image, albeit necessarily a limited one, of the past and present situation of Italian film and advertising industries, and some of the most significant forms of their various mutual intersections. Notwithstanding the important structural differences existing between the Italian film and advertising industries—above all the fact that operators in the former, and not in the latter, have access to public funding—these two sectors appear to be facing two major common struggles. Firstly, both advertising and film production in Italy seem to be somehow caught between a glorious but cumbersome past, and an uncertain future. For Italian professionals, the creativity peaks represented by the golden ages of *Carosello* and auteur cinema are a source of inspiration as well as a difficult blueprint to let go of. Italian critics and scholars have in fact commented on how these traditions may and at times did effectively constitute a limit to the development of new forms of expressions in the field of cinematic (Menarini 2010) and advertising creation (Codeluppi 2013; Mazza 2013). Not to mention how, because of such nostalgic attitudes, past experiences tend to be represented in entirely positive ways which erase or gloss over the problematic aspects that were inherent to those traditions, for example with regard to creative control, and acquiescence to political power and dominant socio-cultural models, as discussed in previous sections.

A second struggle associating Italian film producers and promotional intermediaries is the necessity to deal with limited finances. Being it because of reduced public funds or because of smaller, and ever more fragmented, budgets from advertisers, the long tail of the 2008 global economic crisis continues to significantly affect their work. The financial crunch has repercussions particularly in terms of creative autonomy, as it reduces the practitioners' ability to negotiate the investors' requests, as it emerged, with particular emphasis, from the interviews done with Italian film producers (see Chapter 4). What started off as a temporary difficulty has by now

Conclusions 87

turned into what seems to be a structural condition of the Italian film and advertising industry, or at least a factor with which operators will have to deal with for an indefinite period of time. This poses fundamental questions to researchers, who will increasingly be called upon not only to deconstruct the coping practices put in place by operators of the film and advertising industries, but also to examine the ethos and potential long-term effects of those practices, as critical scholars have recently pointed out (Hamilton, Bodle, and Korin 2017; Hardy, Macrury, and Powell 2018).

In this regard, the data and practitioners' accounts reported in the previous chapter have brought to light some elements that are deserving of a more in-depth discussion and critical evaluation. The next pages will do that by connecting the specific Italian case to analogous practices and trends that have been happening in film and promotional industries around the globe, as well as to some of the major lines of debate that have been engaging critical scholars working on media and advertising. In doing so, we will also endeavour to round off the journey that we started from the distant post-war period and that led us, through inevitable leaps and bounds, up to the present day. We will do so in full awareness that the transformative processes that the book describes, which have brought the Italian film and advertising industries to undergo an increasingly "co-adaptive" (Spurgeon 2008: 2) if not "symbiotic" (Pitteri 2006: 172) development, are far from concluded, and that a continuation and extension of the study on these subjects is necessary.

At the beginning of this book, three peculiarities were established as characterising the Italian media system: a highly concentrated television market, an advertising spending abnormally skewed towards the television medium, and a subaltern relationship of screen-based media to politics and policymaking. These aspects have emerged, acted, and interplayed in different ways across different time periods: initially as a result of factors such as the public broadcaster's monopoly, and the political and cultural influence of the US over Italy; later as an outcome of the savage deregulation of commercial broadcasting, the rise of the media-political empire of Silvio Berlusconi, and the crisis of Italian cinema; and more recently as these aspects arose in the liberalisation of product placement and external tax credit, in the downscaling of direct funding to national cinema, and, more generally, in the promotion of policies and practices of marketisation of Italian film production. In this chronological progression, three main patterns of continuity can be discerned in the relationship between Italian cinema (and screen media more broadly) and advertising. In the pages that follow, we will briefly identify these patterns of continuity and address them within the framework of critical research on media and advertising.

88 *Conclusions*

A friendly separation

The first pattern of continuity that emerged from the account provided in this book has to do with what we might define—borrowing a phrase used by Church historian Philip Schaff to describe the US political and ideological system—as the "friendly separation between church and state" (Schaff 1888: 10) practised by Italian media. In journalistic jargon, the "church and state" metaphor has come to indicate the compartmentalisation between the newsroom and the advertising department, aimed to protect the former from undue pressures from the latter. Even during the years of the public service broadcasting monopoly, while admittedly enforced by meticulous governmental regulations, the separation between editorial and advertising content in Italian television was in fact of a friendly, softer kind. The mere act of allowing RAI to transmit advertising was a significant deviation from the "pure" PBS model, embodied, then and now, by the BBC. Moreover, the peculiar format of *Carosello*, with its extended entertainment bit, the rule whereby each episode could only be aired twice, and the fact that upcoming instalments were advertised in RAI's listing magazine along with regular shows, contributed to what Mara Einstein recently called "content confusion" (Einstein 2016: 7). Content confusion, which is connected to contemporary promotional practices such as native advertising, branded entertainment, and content marketing more generally, stems from the lack of a clear separation between advertising and media content. Such confusion originates from the ambiguous way in which commercial content is framed within the media platform that does not readily present it as advertising, but it also originates from a narrative, visual, and stylistic similarity between the advertisement and the non-commercial media content. Previous sections of this book have looked at how and why Italian cinema has grown to increasingly resemble television advertising, but what is still to be noted are the potential implications of such a phenomenon. Empirical research in marketing and communication shows mixed results concerning the effects that blurring the lines between commercial and non-commercial content has on audience across different platforms, in terms of the evaluation of the brand and the media outlet: see, for example, Van Reijmersdal (2016) for films; Amazeen and Muddiman (2018) and Amazeen and Wojdynski (2018) for news media; Evans et al. (2017) and Hayes et al. (2019) for social media platforms. However, if we look at the "friendly separation" between advertising and media content from the perspective of critical political economy, media ethics, and policy, a number of serious concerns arise. In the case of cinema, and particularly of those film industries such as the Italian and more generally the European ones that benefit from public funding and tax incentives, the incorporation of commercial interests may be seen at odds

Conclusions 89

with the values of artistic integrity and cultural contribution that motivate public support in the first place. As Schejiter (2006) points out, drawing on Habermas' (1989) theory on the erosion of the public sphere, separation of commercial and creative speech is necessary to the truthfulness of the relationship between creators and their audience, as well as to the fair competition within the market for creative contents. Beyond legal and regulatory considerations, scholars have raised the concern of a commodification of culture (Wasko 1994; Wenner 2004), which is higher in the case of cinema, given its previously discussed ability to feed the public imagery, as well as particularly harmful for younger audiences (Wasko 2008).

The American way

Another constant that emerged throughout this book is the persistence of the US as a cultural and industrial reference model for Italian film and advertising practitioners, policymakers, and consumers. As discussed in previous sections, the process of Americanisation of Italian (and more broadly European) culture, in the sense of a massive inflow of US films and television products, as well as a tendency to appropriate and conform to the social models promoted by those media, began in the immediate aftermath of World War II and went on well into the 1980s. Notwithstanding the practices of resistance and negotiation carried out by viewers (on this regard, see the seminal works by Ang, 1985, and D'Acci, 1994), in the early 1990s European television was described as a case of "Dallasification of culture" (De Bens, Kelly, and Bakke 1992), the reference being to the CBS soap opera-turned-cult phenomenon, whose popularity with Italian audiences exploded after Berlusconi's Fininvest, with a foresighted move, acquired it from RAI in 1981. The very European audiovisual media policy, which emerged in those years with the first Television Without Frontiers Directive (1989), was designed and framed in response to the American competitor. The same happened, as we have seen, almost 20 years later with the European Union-wide liberalisation of product placement, which was motivated by the commission's aim to offset competition from US (in fact mostly Hollywood) producers (Reding 2006).

Beyond media markets, policies, and aesthetic models, another important, and relatively less explored, effect of Americanisation is the impact it had on the formation of professional cultures and identities. This aspect emerged clearly during my interviews with Italian film and marketing practitioners. In recounting the origin of the fantasy genre (and brand-integrated) film franchise *Il ragazzo invisibile* (*The invisible boy*) (dir. Salvatores, 2014), one producer I interviewed said that they did not want to give in to the notion that superhero movies, a genre traditionally absent from Italian

90 *Conclusions*

cinema, "were only made in America." (FP 1)[1]. In lamenting the reluctance encountered from some Italian filmmakers to collaborate with advertisers, one promotional intermediary I interviewed ascribed it to the different professional culture existing in the film industry in Italy as opposed to the US:

> It is only in Italy that there is the shame of being associated with a brand. (…) In Italy, for an artist to be associated with a brand it's a form of *marchetta* (sellout). In America, however, the *marchetta* doesn't exist. But that's because in my opinion, and this is really "in my opinion", in America cinema is entertainment, whereas here cinema is art. But we moved forward, didn't we? And now cinema is also other things, it's showbiz, right? There's nothing to be ashamed of. (PI 2)

The comparisons with the US made by the producer and the promotional intermediary, although framed within different discussions, move from the same underlying assumption: that in the US, more than in Italy, there is a professional culture that allows artistic aspirations, commercial goals, and promotional interests to be effectively reconciled so as to satisfy all stakeholders (producers, advertisers, audiences). Practitioners used this type of argument to validate diverse practices—the production of genre movies, the implementation of advertiser-funded operations—which are linked by a strong market drive. The latter is presented as antithetic to the auteur-centred approach that has traditionally dominated Italian and European cinema, and that these practitioners perceive as outdated and in contrast with the current trends of the global film industry.[2] This framework, which revolves around the oppositional pairs of arthouse/popular, culture/industry, Europe/ Hollywood, also emerges in the we/they discourse used by some of my interviewees. Such a discourse raises critical concerns for Italian contemporary film and creative industries. Firstly, it promotes an over-simplistic view of the complex set of drives, logic, and values at play in any context of industrialised cultural production (including Hollywood), and that studies such as those by Caldwell (2008); Hesmondhalgh and Baker (2011); Banks, Conor, and Mayer (2015); and McRobbie (2016) have uncovered. Secondly, such an oppositional framework, whilst simplistic, exposes the problematic and intrinsically conflictual nature of branded entertainment, as it is experienced by the very professionals that participate in its creation and that remain largely overridden by both marketers and policymakers.

Advertising: What's in a name?

A third pattern of continuity that emerged from this work, and that resonates with the one discussed in the previous section, is in the lingering

Conclusions   91

perception of advertising as a negative institution among Italian practitioners. This notion can be seen as the enduring result of the opposition to consumerism affirmed by both the Catholic Church and the Communist Party, around whose ideologies so much of post-war Italian culture was formed. In the case of filmmakers and film producers, such an adversarial attitude is not unexpected, and it is reminiscent of post-Frankfurtian approaches held by many Italian intellectuals and film critics of current and past times (Castellina 2018). What is more surprising, though, is to find similar anti-advertising attitudes also among promotional intermediaries. Such an attitude is visible from my interviews in the vocabulary used by promotional intermediaries, which tends to emphasise the entertainment and cinematic components whilst downplaying advertising:

> Ours is not an advertising *agency*, we don't call ourselves an *agency*: this is an entertainment marketing company. The agency has an advertising notion to it, whereas (…) we work for the production companies (…) and for consumer companies. (PI 1)

> The hardest bit is that in Italy, [advertisers] have not understood what product placement is for. They expect an extended ad, and that's not what we provide. Because product placement is not an extended ad, is not a TV ad. They think it is a cheap ad, whereas it is nothing like that. (PI 2)

The statements of these two promotional intermediaries are at least partially at odds with the reality of the work they do, which is as much at the service of film producers as it is of advertisers: their very remuneration, as we have seen, comes from the former as well as from the latter side. These practitioners' intent to separate their own professional culture and identity from traditional advertising is not an Italian-only phenomenon. As Mara Einstein observed, in reference to the American context, "advertisers no longer think of themselves as producing commercials; they produce 'films'" (Einstein 2016: 10). Such an attitude stems from objective changes affecting marketing and promotional practices over the last decade. The technological, industrial, and cultural convergence that caused the boundaries between marketing, media, and communication businesses to overlap and blur, has pushed practitioners to interrogate the sense and scope of advertising for the 21st century and to adapt their vocabulary accordingly (Macrury 2018). Particularly, with increasing emphasis over the last two decades, advertising practitioners have derived a significant part of legitimacy and self-worth by aligning themselves with the dominant discourse on creative industries and creativity more generally (Nixon 2003). This became apparent in 2011, when the most important global industry event, the annual International

92 *Conclusions*

Advertising Festival, changed its name to Cannes Lions International Festival of Creativity to signal the industry's repositioning in a broader market. In the case of Italian practitioners, though, I argue that the tendency to shy away from the advertising vocabulary has a further, national-specific cause. Advertising has a persuasive, transactional notion to it that is largely viewed as unsexy, at best, and ethically reproachable, at worst. In Italy, all this combines with the long-standing, inextricable association of advertising to television, and more specifically to the cultural and ideological framework of commercial television embodied by Silvio Berlusconi. This is something that most of those working in cultural production tend to (at least publicly) reject. It is nonetheless essential to point out that, regardless of the specific motives, marketers' use of the "rhetoric of creativity" (Bilton 2010: 257) shall not mislead audiences, policymakers, and critics from the fact that what these practitioners do "is advertising, whether marketers call it native advertising, content marketing or anything else" (Einstein 2016: 5). Hence the importance of critical scholarship in media and advertising convergence, to which this book attempted to contribute.

Notes

1　Like in previous Chapter 3, for confidentiality reasons, promotional intermediaries and film producers are here referenced with the letters PI and FP, respectively, followed by numbers in ascending order.
2　The conflict between auteur and popular cinema, arthouse versus commercial production, has always been central to the debate over what constitutes European cinema (as opposed to Hollywood and World cinemas). For comprehensive reviews of the debate, see Jäckel (2003); Harrod, Liz, and Timoshkina (2014); and Liz (2016).

References

AGCM (2017), "Autorità garante della concorrenza e del mercato", *Relazione annuale 2017: Capitolo V – La concorrenza nel settore della distribuzione cinematografica.* www.agcm.it/dotcmsDOC/relazioni-annuali/relazioneannual e2017/cap5_2018.pdf.

AGCOM (2012), "Autorità per le Garanzie nelle Comunicazioni: Indagine Conoscitiva sul Settore della Raccolta Pubblicitaria", *Allegato A alla Delibera n. 551/12/CONS.* www.agcom.it/documents/10179/1/document/bd184d98-cdcd-41e1-b141-9864dcfba8d6.

AGCOM (2013), "Autorità per le Garanzie nelle Comunicazioni. Osservatorio sulla Pubblicità: Prima edizione". www.agcom.it/documents/10179/539991/ Documento+Generico+12-02-2013/5bd50334-c5a2-4318-a830-af67466043 c3?version=1.0.

AGCOM (2017), Autorità per le Garanzie nelle Comunicazioni. Relazione annuale sull'attività svolta e sui programmi di lavoro." www.agcom.it/documents/10 179/8078012/RELAZIONE+ANNUALE+2017_documento+completo.pdf/20 21e7ba-8250-4239-9a46-5d82fdbf702c

AGCOM (2018), "Autorità per le Garanzie nelle Comunicazioni. Relazione annuale sull'attività svolta e sui programmi di lavoro." www.agcom.it/documents/10 179/11258925/Relazione+annuale+2018/24dc1cc0-27a7-4ddd-9db2-cf3fc 03f91d2

Alberoni, F. (1968), *Pubblicità, Televisione e Società nell'Italia del Miracolo Economico*, Armando editore.

Amazeen, M., and A. R. Muddiman (2018), "Saving media or trading on trust? The effects of native advertising on audience perceptions of legacy and online news publishers", *Digital Journalism*, 6(2): pp. 176–195.

Amazeen, M., and B. W. Wojdynski (2018), "The effects of disclosure format on native advertising recognition and audience perceptions of legacy and online news publishers", *Journalism: Theory, Practice and Criticism.* https://doi. org/10.1177/1464884918754829

Amaro Ramazzotti (1985), *Milano Da Bere* [advertisement on Italian national television].

94 References

Ambrosino, P. (2004), "L'anima del commercio e l'anima del servizio pubblico. La pubblicità televisiva nei regolamenti RAI-SACIS", in Canova, G. (ed.), *Dreams. I sogni degli italiani in cinquant'anni di pubblicità televisiva*, Bruno Mondadori: pp. 293–303.

Anderson, B. (1983), *Imagined Communities: Reflections on the Origin and Spread of Nationalism*, Verso.

Ang, I. (1985), *Watching Dallas. Soap Opera and the Melodramatic Imagination*, Routledge.

ANICA (2008), "I quaderni dell'ANICA – N.1 product placement". www.anica.it/online/attachments/018_quaderno1.pdf.

ANICA (2017), "Tutti i numeri del cinema italiano – anno 2017". www.anica.it/documentazione-e-dati-annuali-2/tutti-i-numeri-del-cinema-italiano-anno-2017.

Annunziato, S., and F. Fiumara (2015), "Targeting the parents through the children in the golden age of Italian television advertising: The case of Carosello", *Journal of Italian Cinema and Media Studies*, 3(1–2): pp. 11–26.

Arvidsson, A. (2003), *Marketing Modernity: Italian Advertising from Fascism to Postmodernity*, Routledge.

Banks, M., B. Conor, and V. Mayer (eds.) (2015), *Production Studies, The Sequel! Cultural Studies of Global Media Industries*, Routledge.

Barra, L., and M. Scaglioni (2017), "Il ruolo della televisione nel sostegno al cinema italiano", in Cucco, M., and G. Manzoli (eds.), *Il cinema di Stato. Finanziamento pubblico ed economia simbolica nel cinema italiano contemporaneo*, Il Mulino: pp. 85–125.

Barthes, R. (1977), *Image/Music/Text*, Hill and Wang.

Beeton, S. (2005), *Film-Induced Tourism*, Channel View Publications.

Bennett, L. (1998), "The UnCivic culture: Communication, identity, and the rise of lifestyle politics", *PS: Political Science and Politics*, 31–34: pp. 740–761.

Bilton, C. (2010), "Manageable creativity", *International Journal of Cultural Policy*, 16(3): pp. 255–269.

Boddy, W. (1990), *Fifties Television. The Industry and Its Critics*, University of Illinois Press.

Bondanella, P., and F. Pacchioni (2017), *A History of Italian Cinema* (2nd edition), Bloomsbury.

Bourdon, J. (2001), *Introduzione ai Media*, Il Mulino.

Brevini, B. (2013), *Public Service Broadcasting Online: A Comparative European Policy Study of PSB 2.0*, Palgrave Macmillan.

Brigida, F., P. Baudi Di Vesme, and L. Francia,(2004), *Media e pubblicità in Italia* (3rd edition), Franco Angeli.

Brunetta, G. P. (2003), *Guida alla Storia Del Cinema Italiano 1905–2003*, Einaudi.

Burke, F. (ed.) (2017), *A Companion to Italian Cinema*, Wiley Blackwell.

Caldwell, J. T. (2008), *Production Culture. Industrial Reflexivity and Critical Practice in Film and Television*, Duke University Press.

Canova, G. (ed.) (2004), *Dreams. I sogni degli italiani in cinquant'anni di pubblicità televisiva*, Bruno Mondadori.

Canova, G. (2016), *Quo chi? Di cosa ridiamo quando ridiamo di Checco Zalone*, Sagoma.

References 95

Castellina, L. (2018), "Bertolucci, gli intellettuali e la debolezza della sinistra", *Il Manifesto*, 27 November 2018.

Cigognetti, L., and P. Sorlin (2007), "Italy. Cinema and television: Collaborators and threat", in Ostrowska, D., and G. Roberts (eds.), *European Cinemas in the Television Age*, Edinburgh University Press: pp. 41–54.

Cinetel (2016), Annuario Cinetel 2016, www.cinetel.it/pages/studi_e_ricerche.php

Codeluppi, V. (2013), *Storia della pubblicità italiana*, Carocci.

Corsi, B. (2001), *Con qualche dollaro in meno. Storia economica del cinema italiano*, Editori riuniti.

Corsi, B. (2003), "Il cinema italiano in cifre", in Brunetta, G. P. (ed.), *Guida alla storia del cinema italiano 1905-2003*, Einaudi: pp. 825–838.

Corsi, B. (2012), *Produzione e produttori*, Il castoro.

Corti, G. (2004), *Occulta Sarà Tua Sorella! Pubblicità, Product Placement, Persuasione: Dalla Psicologia Subliminale Ai Nuovi Media*, Castelvecchi.

Costa, A. (2010), *Federico Fellini La Dolce Vita*, Il castoro.

Cucco, M., and G. Manzoli (eds.) (2017), *Il cinema di Stato. Finanziamento pubblico ed economia simbolica nel cinema italiano contemporaneo*, Il Mulino.

Cucco, M., and G. Richeri (2013), *Il Mercato delle Location Cinematografiche*, Marsilio.

Cucco, M., and M. Scaglioni (2013), "Dico Parolacce, Incasso e Finisco Su Sky: TV, Cinema, Di Nuovo Tv. Il Viaggio Del Comico Nel XXI Secolo", *Bianco e Nero*, 575, January/April 2013: pp. 30–40.

Cushion, S. (2012), *Television Journalism*, SAGE.

D'Acci, J. (1994), *Defining Women: Television and the Case of Cagney and Lacey*, The University of North Carolina Press.

Dagnino, G. (2014), "It's a branded new world: The influence of Regional policy and product placement upon contemporary Italian film narrative", in Pearson, R., and A. Smith (eds.), *Storytelling in the Media Convergence Age: Exploring Screen Narratives*, Palgrave Macmillan: pp. 93–107.

Davis, A. (2013), *Promotional Cultures: The Rise and Spread of Advertising, Public Relations, Marketing and Branding*, Polity.

De Bens, E., and H. de Smaele (2001), "The inflow of American television fiction on European broadcasting channels revisited", *European Journal of Communication*, 16(1): pp. 51–76.

De Bens, E., M. Kelly, and M. Bakke (1992), "Television content: Dallasification of culture", in Siune, K., and W. Truetzschler (eds.), *Dynamics of Media Politics*, Sage: pp. 75–150.

De Mauro, T. (1968), "Lingua parlata e TV", in De Mauro, T., et al. (eds.), *Televisione e Vita Italiana*, Torino: ERI: pp. 247–294.

Di Mauro, V. (2010), "Why every company is a media company", Every Company Is a Media Company, March 2010. https://www.everycompanyisamediacompany.com/every-company-is-a-media-/2010/03/why-every-company-is-a-media-company.html.

Dorfles, P. (1998), *Carosello*, Il Mulino.

96 *References*

EAO (European Audiovisual Observatory) (2017), "The EU Online Advertising Market – Update 2017," Strasbourg, 2017. https://rm.coe.int/the-eu-online-advertising-market-update-2017/168078f2b3.

Eco, U. (1990), "A Guide to the Neo-Television of the 1980s", in Baranski, Z. G., and R. Lumley (eds.), *Culture and Conflict in Postwar Italy. Essays on Mass and Popular Culture*, Palgrave Macmillan: pp. 245–255.

Ellwood, D. (1992), *Rebuilding Europe: Western Europe, America and Postwar Reconstruction*, Routledge.

Ellwood, D., and R. Kroes (1994), *Hollywood in Europe: Experiences of a Cultural Hegemony*, VU University Press.

Ercole, P., D. Treveri Gennari, and C. G. O'Rawe (2017), "Mapping cinema memories: Emotional geographies of cinema-going in Rome in the 1950s", *Memory Studies*, 10(1): pp. 63–77.

Falk, P. (1997), "The Benetton-Toscani effect: Testing the limits of conventional advertising", in Nava, M., A. Blake, I. MacRury, and B. Richards (eds.), *Buy This Book: Studies in Advertising and Consumption*, Routledge: pp. 64–83.

Fanchi, M. G. (2002), *Identità mediatiche. Televisione e cinema nelle storie di vita di due generazioni di spettatori*, Franco Angeli.

Fanchi, M. G., and E. Mosconi (2002), *Spettatori. Forme di consumo e pubblici del cinema in Italia. 1930–1960*, Marsilio.

Fiorelli, P. (2016), "I 50 film Italiani più visti al cinema dal 1950 a oggi", *TV Sorrisi e Canzoni*, 20 January 2016. www.sorrisi.com/cinema/film-piu-visti/classifica-50-film-italiani-piu-visti-al-cinema/.

Fofi, G. (2016), "L'Italia malinconica e meschina di Checco Zalone", *Internazionale*, 11 January 2016. www.internazionale.it/opinione/goffredo-fofi/2016/01/11/quo-vado-checco-zalone-recensione.

Einstein, M. (2016), *Black Ops Advertising*, OR Books.

Evans, N. J., J. Phua, J. Lim, and H. Jun (2017), "Disclosing Instagram influencer advertising: The effects of disclosure language on advertising recognition, attitudes, and behavioral intent", *Journal of Interactive Advertising*, 17(2): pp. 138–149.

Forgacs, D. (1990), *Italian Culture in the Industrial Era 1880–1980. Cultural Industries, Politics and the Public*, Manchester University Press.

Forgacs, D. (2000), *L'industrializzazione della cultura italiana (1880–2000)*, Il Mulino.

Forgacs, D., and S. Gundle (2007), *Mass Culture and Italian Society from Fascism to the Cold War*, Indiana University Press.

Fuchs, C. (2003), "Globalization and self-organization in the knowledge-based society", *TripleC: Communication, Capitalism and Critique. Open Access Journal for a Global Sustainable Information Society*, 1(1): pp. 1–52.

Galt, R. (2013), "The prettiness of Italian cinema", in Bayman, L., and S. Rigoletto (eds.), *Popular Italian Cinema*, Palgrave Macmillan.

Gambetti, R. C., and G. Graffigna (2010), "The concept of engagement: A systematic analysis of the ongoing marketing debate", *International Journal of Market Research*, 52(6): pp. 801–826.

References   97

Ginosar, A. (2012), "Change and divergence in regulatory regimes: A comparative study of product placement regulation", in Just, N., and M. Puppis (eds.), *Trends in Communication Policy Research: New Theories, Methods and Subjects, Intellectica*: pp. 95–115.

Ginsborg, P. (1990), *A History of Contemporary Italy. Society and Politics 1943–1988*, Penguin Books.

Girelli, E. (2009), *Beauty and the Beast. Italianness in British Cinema*, Intellect Books.

Giroux, H. A. (1994), "Consuming social change: The 'United Colors of Benetton'", *Cultural Critique*, 26, Winter 1993–1994: pp. 5–32.

Grainge, P. (ed.) (2011), *Ephemeral Media. Transitory Screen Culture from Television to YouTube*, Bloomsbury.

Grainge, P., and C. Johnson (2015), *Promotional Screen Industries*, Routledge.

Grasso, A. (2000), *La scatola nera della pubblicità*, Sipra.

Gundle, S. (1986), "L'Americanizzazione del Quotidiano. Televisione e Consumismo nell'Italia degli Anni Cinquanta", *Quaderni Storici*, 21(62–2): pp. 561–594.

Gundle, S. (2000), *Between Hollywood and Moscow. The Italian Communists and the Challenge of Mass Culture, 1943–1991*, Duke University Press.

Habermas, J. (1989), *The Structural Transformation of the Public Sphere: An Enquiry into a Category of Bourgeois Society*, MIT Press.

Hallin, D. C., and P. Mancini (2004), *Comparing Media System. Three Models of Media and Politics*, Cambridge University Press.

Hamilton, J. F., R. Bodle, and E. Korin (eds.) (2017), *Explorations in Critical Studies of Advertising*, Routledge.

Hardy, J. (2010), *Cross-Media Promotion*, Peter Lang.

Hardy, J. (2011), "Mapping commercial intertextuality: HBO's true blood", *Convergence*, 17(1): pp. 7–17.

Hardy, J. (2013), "The changing relationship between media and marketing", in Powell, H. (ed.), *Promotional Culture and Convergence: Markets, Methods, Media*, Routledge: pp.125–150.

Hardy, J., I. Macrury, and H. Powell (eds.) (2018), *The Advertising Handbook* (4th edition), Routledge.

Harrod, M., M. Liz, and A. Timoshkina (eds.) (2014), *The Europeanness of European Cinema. Identity, Meaning, Globalization*, I.B. Tauris.

Hayes, J. L., G. Golan, B. Britt, and J. Applequist (2019), "How advertising relevance and consumer–Brand relationship strength limit disclosure effects of native ads on Twitter", *International Journal of Advertising*, April 2019: pp. 1–35.

Hesmondhalgh, D., and S. Baker (2011), *Creative Labour: Media Work in Three Cultural Industries*, Routledge.

Hibberd, M. (2008), *The Media in Italy*, Open University Press.

Holdaway, D. (2017), "La rete sociale del cinema di interesse culturale", in Cucco, M., and G. Manzoli (eds.), *Il cinema di stato. Finanziamento pubblico ed economia simbolica nel cinema italiano contemporaneo*, Il Mulino: pp. 127–169.

Hope, W. (2005), *Italian Cinema: New Directions*, Peter Lang.

98 References

ISTAT (1951), "Censimento generale della popolazione", 4 Novembre, Istituto nazionale di Statistica.

ISTAT (1981), "Censimento generale della popolazione", 25 Ottobre, Istituto nazionale di Statistica.

ISTAT (2013), "Internet @Italia 2013".

Jäckel, A. (2003), *European Film Industries*, British Film Institute.

Jenkins, H. (2006), *Convergence Culture. Where Old and New Media Collide*, New York University Press.

La Repubblica (May 21, 1985), "Fellini denuncia Canale 5 per gli spot pubblicitari" https://ricerca.repubblica.it/repubblica/archivio/repubblica/1985/05/21/fellini-denuncia-canale-per-gli-spot-pubblicitari.html.

La Repubblica (August 1, 1985), Fellini non ferma Berlusconi 'ma sugli spot serve una legge', https://ricerca.repubblica.it/repubblica/archivio/repubblica/1985/08/01/fellini-non-ferma-berlusconi-ma-sugli-spot.html.

Lehu, J.-M. (2007), *Branded Entertainment. Product Placement & Brand Strategy in the Entertainment Business*, Kogan Page.

Leonida, L., D. Maimone Ansaldo Patti, and P. Navarra (2015), "The impact of political calculus on the reform of institutions and growth: Old and new examples", in Mammone, A., E. Parini, and G. A. Veltri (eds.), *The Routledge Handbook of Contemporary Italy: History, Politics, Society*, Routledge: pp. 262–271.

Liz, M. (2016), *Euro-Visions: Europe in Contemporary Cinema*, Bloomsbury.

Lugmayr, A., and C. Dal Zotto (eds.) (2016), *Media Convergence Handbook*. Vols. 1 and 2, Springer.

Macrury, I. (2018), "What is an advertising agency in the twenty-first century", in Hardy, J., I. Macrury, and H. Powell (eds.), *The Advertising Handbook* (4th edition), Routledge, https://doi.org/10.4324/9781315558646-12.

Maltese, C. (2011), "Perché i ricchi e scemi non fanno più ridere/Il cinepanettone non piace più", *La Repubblica*, December 27. https://ricerca.repubblica.it/repubblica/archivio/repubblica/2011/12/27/perche-ricchi-scemi-non-fanno-piu-ridere.html.

Mancini, P. (2011), *Between Commodification and Lifestyle Politics: Does Silvio Berlusconi Provide a New Model of Politics for the 21st Century?*, Reuters Institute for the Study of Journalism.

Marglin, S., and J. Schor (1990), *The Golden Age of Capitalism: Reinterpreting the Postwar Experience*, Clarendon Press.

Mattelart, A. (1991), *Advertising International. The Privatisation of Public Space*, Routledge.

Mazza, G. (2013), "Nostalgia di Carosello?", *Doppiozero*, May 22. www.doppiozero.com/rubriche/1468/201305/nostalgia-di-carosello.

Mazzoleni, G. (1995), "Towards a 'Videocracy'? Italian political communication at a turning point", *European Journal of Communication*, 10(3): pp. 291–319.

McKinsey & Company (2013), "Global media report 2013. Global industry overview". www.mckinsey.com/~/media/mckinsey/dotcom/client_service/Media%20and%20Entertainment/PDFs/Global_Media_Report_2013.ashx.

McRobbie, A. (2016), *Be Creative. Making a Living in the New Culture Industries*, Polity Press.

References 99

Menarini, R. (2010), *Il cinema dopo il cinema. Dieci idee sul cinema italiano 2001–2010*, Le Mani.

MIBAC (2017), "Relazione sull'utilizzazione del Fondo Unico per lo Spettacolo e sull'andamento complessivo dello spettacolo (Anno 2017)". www.spettacolod alvivo.beniculturali.it/index.php/trasparenza/doc_download/2351-relazione-f us-anno-2017-on-line.

MiBACT (2016), "Tutti i numeri del cinema italiano," Anno 2016. www.cinema .beniculturali.it/Notizie/4483/67/tutti-i-numeri-del-cinema-italiano-2016/.

Miller, T., et al. (2004), *Global Hollywood 2*, Bloomsbury.

Minuz, A. (2015a), *Political Fellini: Journey to the End of Italy*, Berghahan.

Minuz, A. (2015b), "Solo la commedia può dire la verità, quella di Quo vado? è terrificante e vera", *Il Foglio*, December 29. www.ilfoglio.it/cultura/2015/12/29/news/solo-la-co mmedia-puo-dire-la-verita-quella-di-quo-vado-e-terrificante-e-vera-91062/.

Montanari, F. (2007), "Al di là della sala cinematografica", in Casetti, F., and S. Salvemini (eds.), *È tutto un altro film. Più coraggio e più idee per il cinema italiano*, Egea: pp. 53–84.

Montanari, F., and A. Usai (2002), "La squadra artistica e creativa", in Salvemini, S. (ed.), *Il cinema impresa possibile. La sfida del cambiamento per il cinema italiano*, Egea: pp. 57–84.

Monteleone, F. (1992), *Storia della radio e della televisione in Italia. Società, politica, strategie, programmi 1922–1992*, Marsilio.

Napoli, P. M. (2011), *Audience Evolution. New Technologies and the Transformation of Media Audiences*, Columbia University Press.

Nelli, R. P. (ed.) (2013), *Product Placement Made in Italy. Una visione d'insieme dell'esperienza italiana dal 2004 al 2011*, Fondazione Ente dello Spettacolo.

Nelli, R. P. and L. Patruno (2014), *L'evoluzione del product placement Made in Italy tra il 2005 e il 2014*, Fondazione Ente dello Spettacolo

Nicoli, M. (2011), "Entrepreneurs and the state in the Italian film industry, 1919–1935", *The Business History Review*, 85(4): pp. 775–798.

Nicoli, M. (2017), *The Rise and Fall of the Italian Film Industry*, Routledge.

Nixon, S. (2003), *Advertising Cultures: Gender, Commerce, Creativity*, SAGE.

Ofcom (2016), "Communications market report 2016", August 4. www.ofcom.org. uk/__data/assets/pdf_file/0024/26826/cmr_uk_2016.pdf.

Ofcom (2019), "The Ofcom broadcasting code. Section nine: Commercial references in television programming", January 2019. www.ofcom.org.uk/__data/assets/ pdf_file/0018/132084/Broadcast-Code-Section-9.pdf.

O'Leary, A. (2010), "Italian cinema and the 'anni di piombo'", *Journal of European Studies*, 40(3): pp. 243–257.

O'Leary, A. (2011), "The phenomenology of the cinepanettone", *Italian Studies*, 66(3): pp. 431–443.

Olsberg, J., and A. Barnes (2014), "Impact analysis of fiscal incentive schemes supporting film and audiovisual production in Europe", European Audiovisual Observatory Report.

Ortner, S. (2009), "Studying Sideways: Ethnographic Access in Hollywood", in Mayer, V., Banks, M. J. and J. T. Caldwell (eds.), *Production Studies. Cultural Studies of Media Industries*, Routledge: pp. 175-189.

100 *References*

Ortoleva, Peppino (2008), "La televisione italiana 1974–2002: dall' 'anarchie italienne' al duopolio imperfetto", in Castronovo, V., and N. Tranfaglia (eds.), *La stampa italiana nell'età della TV* (3rd edition), Laterza: pp. 95–177.

Padovani, C. (2005), *A Fatal Attraction: Public Television and Politics in Italy*, Rowman & Littlefield.

Padovani, C. (2015), "Media and democracy", inMammone, A., E. Parini, and G. A. Veltri (eds.), *The Routledge Handbook of Contemporary Italy: History, Politics, Society*, Routledge: pp. 127–134.

Pasolini, P. P. (1975), *Scritti corsari*, Garzanti.

Pitteri, D. (2006), *La pubblicità in Italia. Dal dopoguerra a oggi*, Laterza.

Ranalli, A. (2008), "Sì al Product Placement, questa la direttiva che sconvolgerà la TV", *Italia Oggi*, July 9. www.italiaoggi.it/archivio/la-direttiva-che-sconvolgera -la-tv-1559248.

Reding, V. (2006), "Advertising as the cornerstone of a strong European media landscape", *Speech 06/506 Given at the Annual Congress of Swiss Press, St. Moritz*, September 15, http://europa.eu/rapid/press-release_SPEECH-06-506 _en.htm.

R&S Mediobanca (2019), Focus R&S sul settore TV (2013-2018), www.mbres.it/si tes/default/files/resources/Presentazione%20TV%202018.pdf

Riall, L. (1994), *The Italian Risorgimento. State, Society and National Unification*, Routledge, London.

Richeri, G. (1990), "Hard times for public service broadcasting: The RAI in the age of commercial competition", in Baranski, Z. G., and R. Lumley (eds.), *Culture and Conflict in Postwar Italy. Essays on Mass and Popular Culture*, Palgrave Macmillan: pp. 256–269.

Richeri, G. (2009), "Le tre fasi della TV in Italia", in Bonomi, A., and A. Abruzzese (eds.), *La cultura in Italia*, Utet: pp. 475–493.

Roberts, K. (2004), *Lovemarks: The Future Beyond Brands*, Powerhouse Books.

Sandfeld Jakobsen, S. (2013), "Denmark. Reintroduction of ban against product placement", *Iris*, 2013-6(1/15). http://merlin.obs.coe.int/article.php?id =14319.

Scarpellini, E. (2004), "Shopping American-style: The arrival of the supermarket in postwar Italy", *Enterprise and Society*, 5(4): pp. 625–668.

Scarpellini, E. (2011), *Material Nation. A Consumer's History of Modern Italy*, Oxford University Press.

Schaff, P. (1888), *Church and State in the United States*, Charles Scribner's Sons.

Schejter, A. (2006), "Art thou for us, Or for our adversaries? Communicative action and the regulation of product placement: A comparative study and a tool for analysis", *Tulane Journal of International and Comparative Law*, 15(89): pp. 90–119.

Schlesinger, P. (1991), "Media, the political order and national identity", *Media, Culture and Society*, 13(3): pp. 297–308.

Scotto Lavina, E. (2015), *Il Cantiere Televisivo Italiano. Progetto Struttura Canone*, Lampi di stampa.

Segreto, L. (2002), "Changing a low consumption society. The impact of US advertising methods and techniques in Italy", in Kipping, M., and N. Tiratsoo

References 101

(eds.), *Americanisation in 20th Century Europe,* Volume 2: *Economics, Culture, Politics,* Centre de recherche sur l'histoire de l'Europe du Nord-Ouest, Université Charles de Gaulle, Lille: pp. 75–91.

Semino, E., and M. Masci (1996), "Politics is football: Metaphor in the discourse of Silvio Berlusconi in Italy", *Discourse and Society,* 7(2): pp. 243–269.

Senato delle Repubblica (1988), 8° Commissione permanente (lavori pubblici, comunicazioni), "Indagine conoscitiva sull'emittenza radiotelevisiva e sulle connessioni con I settori dell'editoria e dell'informazione", 10° Resoconto stenografico, Seduta del, 20 Ottobre 1988. www.senato.it/service/PDF/PDFS erver/DF/258407.pdf.

Shandley, R. (2009), *Runaway Romances. Hollywood's Postwar Tour of Europe,* Temple University Press.

SIAE (1955), Società italiana degli autori ed editori, Statistica documentazione annuario dello spettacolo 1955, www.siae.it/it/chi-siamo/lo-spettacolo-cifre/losservatorio-dello-spettacolo

SIAE (1975), Società italiana degli autori ed editori, Statistica documentazione annuario dello spettacolo 1975, www.siae.it/it/chi-siamo/lo-spettacolo-cifre/losservatorio-dello-spettacolo

Sorlin, P. (1996), *Italian National Cinema,* Routledge: pp. 1896–1996.

Spurgeon, C. (2008), *Advertising and New Media,* Routledge.

Sznajder, M. (1995), "Italy's right-wing government: Legitimacy and criticism", *International Affairs,* 71(1): pp. 83–102.

Tobia, S. (2008), *Advertising America: The United States information service in Italy (1945–1956),* LED Edizioni Universitarie.

Tomasi, G. (2004), *Il cinema e la misurazione delle performance,* Egea.

Treveri Gennari, D. (2009), *Post-War Italian Cinema: American Intervention, Vatican Interests,* Routledge.

Treveri Gennari, D., C. G. O'Rawe, and D. Hipkins (2011), "In search of Italian cinema audiences in the 1940s and 1950s: Gender, genre and national identity", *Participations: Journal of Audience & Reception Studies,* 8(2): pp. 539–553.

Treveri Gennari, D., and J. Sedgwick (2015), "Memories in context: The social and economic function of cinema in 1950s Rome", *Film History,* 27(2): pp. 76–104.

Turrini, D. (2016), "Checco Zalone, per "Quo vado" record di incassi ma nella classifica dei film più visti di sempre è solo 43esimo", *Il fatto quotidiano,* January 21. www.ilfattoquotidiano.it/2016/01/21/checco-zalone-per-il-record-d i-quo-vado-deve-ringraziare-laumento-del-prezzo-dei-biglietti-solo-43esimo-tra-i-film-piu-visti-della-storia/2394331/.

UNESCO (1957), "World illiteracy at mid-century. A statistical study", *Buchdruckerei Winterthur Ag.* http://unesdoc.unesco.org/images/0000/000029/002930eo.pdf.

van Reijmersdal, E. A. (2016), "Disclosing brand placements in movies: Effects of disclosure type and movie involvement on attitudes", *Journal of Media Psychology: Theories, Methods, and Applications,* 28(2): pp. 78–87.

Wagstaff, C. (1995), "Italy in the post-war international cinema market", in Duggan, C., and C. Wagstaff (eds.), *Italy in the Cold War: Politics, Culture and Society 1948–1958,* Berg.

102 *References*

Wasko, J. (1994), *Hollywood in the Information Age. Beyond the Silver Screen*, Polity Press.

Wasko, J. (2008), "The commodification of youth culture", in Drotner, K., and S. Livingstone (eds.), *The International Handbook of Children, Media and Culture*, SAGE: pp. 460–474.

Wenner, L. A. (2004), "On the ethics of product placement in media entertainment", in M.-L. Galician (ed.), *Handbook of Product Placement in the Mass Media. New Strategies in Marketing Theory, Practice, Trends and Ethics*, Haworth Press: pp. 101–132.

Index

01 Distribution 2, 36, 59
1975 Reform Law 45
2007/65/EC Audiovisual Media Services Without Frontiers Directive 67
2010/13/EU, Audiovisual Media Services Directive 2, 67

ad hoc scenes, product placement 78–80
admissions 57–58
advertisers 2–6
advertising: anti-interruptions campaign 53; *Carosello* (Carousel) 21–24; through cinema 27–32; as a negative institution 90–92; spot advertising 49–50; television 48–52
advertising agencies 16–17
advertising "blocks" 50
Advertising Code of Conduct (*Codice di autodisciplina pubblicitaria*) 17
advertising communication 62
advertising modernity 16–18
advertising revenue 64–65
AGCOM (Authority for Communications Guarantees) 47; product placement 66
agreements for product placement 72
AIART (Italian Association of Radio and Television Listeners) 51
Alberoni, Francesco 9–10
Amaro Ramazzotti 41–42
Amazeen, Michelle 88
An American in Rome (Steno, 1954) 13
Americanisation 11
American-style consumerism 11

American-style economic boom 13–18
American way, impact on Italian film 89–90
Anderson, Benedict 9
Andreotti, Giulio 27
Andreotti law 26–27, 59
Angiolini, Ambra 45
ANICA (National Association of Film Industries) 26
Annabella 53
"anthropological revolution" 18
anti-interruptions campaign 53
Antonioni, Michelangelo 25
Apple 62
April (1998) 55
Arvidsson, Adam 42
attendance at cinema 57–58
Audiovisual Media Services (AVMS) 67
Auditel 50–51
August Vacation (Ferie d'agosto) (Virzì, 1996) 55
Authority for Communications Guarantees (AGCOM) 47
AVMS (Audiovisual Media Services) 67

Bellucci, Monica 53
Benetton clothing 43
Benigni, Roberto 53
Bennett, Lance 41
Benvenuto Presidente! (Welcome Mr. President!) (Milani, 2013) 79
Berlusconi, Silvio 5–6, 38–40, 68, 87; advertising revenue 49; commercial breaks 55; Fininvest 46

104 *Index*

"Berlusconi decree" 5
Berlusconism 56
Bernabei, Ettore 20
Bertolucci, Bernardo 25
Blandini, Gaetano 69
Bobbio, Norberto 40
Boldi, Massimo 43
Bologna massacre 38
Bonaccorti, Enrica 45
Bondanella, Peter 25
Bozzetto, Bruno 23
branded content 77–84
branded entertainment 22
brands: impact of being in films 77–84;
   lovemarks 62; marketing 71–76;
   product placement *see* product
   placement
"Bribesgate" (*Tangentopoli*) 35,
   38–39
broadcasting industry, advertisers 3–4
broadcasting reform law (1975) 20
Burghy 42

The Caiman (2006) 55
Camelot 73
Campanile sera ("It's a knockout,"
   1959-1962) 19
Cannes Lions International Festival of
   Creativity 91–92
Carosello (Carousel) 4–5, 11–12,
   21–24, 44; Moplen 15
censorship, *Carosello* (Carousel) 23
Christian Democracy Party 11, 37, 39;
   Mamma RAI 19–20
"Christmas holidays" (*Vacanze di
   Natale*) (Vanzina, 1983) 43
"Christmas holidays in Cortina"
   (*Vacanze di Natale a Cortina*)
   (Parenti, 2011) 56
"church and state" metaphor 88–89
cinegiornale (propaganda newsreel) 28
cinema attendance 57–58
Cinema General Directorate 26–27
cinemagoing 24
Cinema Paradiso (Tornatore) 57
cinepanettoni 42–43, 56
Coca-Cola 62
Codice di autodisciplina pubblicitaria
   (Advertising Code of Conduct) 17
Colombo, Fulvia 18

The Commander and the Stork (*Il
   comandante e la cicogna*) (Soldini,
   2012) 79
commedia all'Italiana (Italian-style
   comedy) 13, 30
commercial breaks 53–54
commercial televisions 42, 50–51
"Committee for the defense of Italian
   cinema" 26
consumerism 34–35; American-style
   consumerism 11
content confusion 88
"Content is king" 62
continuity: advertising 90–92;
   American way 89–90; "friendly
   separation between church and state"
   88–89
convergence 36
COOP 79
Copernican revolution 49
Corriere della sera 15
Craxi, Bettino 5, 38, 39
creative control, product placement
   77–84
criticism of cinema 36–37

D'Alatri, Alessandro 44, 55
"Dallasification of culture" 89
D'Amico, Suso Cecchi 53
Danone 53
D'Azeglio, Massimo 9
DeeJay Television 42
Dell'Utri, Marcello 40
Delon, Alain 53
Democratic Party of the Left (PDS) 54
De Sica Christian 43–44
Directive 2010/13/EU 67
Di Saronno liqueur 79, 83
Discovery Channel 47
Discovery Italia 47
divorce 20
Dolce & Gabbana 53
dolcevita 31
Dorfles, P. 22, 23
dubbing tax 26

Eco, Umberto 45, 52
economic boom 13–18; second
   economic miracle 41
economic decline 43

Index 105

editing phase, product placement 82–84
Einstein, Mara 88, 91
Ellwood, David 13
engagement marketing 62
entertainment marketing companies 72–75
EU (European Union), product placement 66–68
EU Directive 2018/1808 67
European Recovery Programme (Marshall Plan) 11, 13
Evans, N. J. 88

Fascism, cinegiornale (propaganda newsreel) 28
Fede, Emilio 51
Federazione Italiana della Pubblicità ("Italian Federation of Advertising") 17
Fellini, Federico 25, 30, 53
Ferie d'agosto (*August Vacation*) (Virzì, 1996) 55
Filmauro 72
film producers, product placement 75–76
film production market 68–70
film-rotocalco (tabloid films) 30
films: *An American in Rome* (Steno, 1954) 13; *April* (1998) 55; *August Vacation* (*Ferie d'agosto*) (Virzì, 1996) 55; *Benvenuto Presidente!* (*Welcome Mr. President!*) (Milani, 2013) 79; *The Caiman* (Moretti, 2006) 55; *Cinema Paradiso* (Tornatore) 57; golden age of cinema 24–32; *The Great Beauty* (*La Grande Bellezza*) (Sorrentino, 2013) 83–84; *The Icicle Thief* ("Ladri di saponette," Nichetti, 1989) 52–53; *Il comandante e la cicogna* (*The Commander and the Stork*) (Soldini, 2012) 79; *Il ragazzo invisibile* (*The invisible boy*) (Salvatores, 2014) 89; *Il ricco, il povero e il maggiordomo* ("The rich, the poor and the butler") (Bertacca, 2014) 78; impact of brands 77–84; impact of US 89–90; *La Dolce Vita* (Fellini, 1960) 30; *Loro* act 1 (2018) 55; *Loro* act 2 (2018) 55; marketing 71–76; *Mediterraneo* (Salvatores, 1991) 57; *Quo Vado?* ("Where am I going?") (Nunziante, 2016) 1; *Roman Holiday* (Wyler, 1953) 29; *Scusate se esisto* ("Sorry if I exist") 80; tabloid films 30; *This Must Be the Place* (Sorrentino, 2011) 81–82; US films 29; *Vacanze di Natale* ("Christmas holidays") (Vanzina, 1983) 43; *Vacanze di Natale a Cortina* ("Christmas holidays in Cortina") (Parenti, 2011) 56; "Vai, paparazzo!" (Wenders, 2015) 31
film theatres 35–36
final cut, product placement 82–84
financial crisis (2007-2008) 64–65
Fininvest 5, 45, 46, 51, 89
FIP (*Federazione Italiana della Pubblicità*, "Italian Federation of Advertising") 17
First Republic, end of 39
Fondo Unico per lo spettacolo (FUS) 65
"Forbidden to forbid" 54
forced loans 26
foreign advertising agencies 16–17
Foremski, Tom 62
Forgacs, D. 35, 49
Forza Italia 38–40
"Forza Italia clubs" 40
Franceschini, Dario 1
free-to-air (FTA) 3
"friendly separation between church and state" 88–89
FTA (free-to-air) 3
funding 86–87; national film funding 58–60, 65, 71
FUS (*Fondo Unico per lo spettacolo*) 58, 65

Garrone, Matteo 55
Gasparri law 48
Gates, Bill 62
Giusti, Marco 37
global financial crisis (2007-2008) 64–65
Godard, Jean-Luc 24, 56
gold 12
golden age of cinema 24–32

106   Index

The Great Beauty (*La Grande Bellezza*) (Sorrentino, 2013) 83–84
Guadagnino, Luca 55

Hardy, Jonathan 63
Hayes, Jameson L. 88
Herfindahl-Hirschman index 3, 48
'hold-all' programme 45
"Hollywood on the Tiber" 30
home videos 58

IBEC (International Basic Economy Corporation) 15
The Icicle Thief ("Ladri di saponette") (Nichetti, 1989) 52–53
Il comandante e la cicogna (*The Commander and the Stork*) (Soldini, 2012) 79
Il musichiere ("The music maker") 19
Il ragazzo invisible (*The invisible boy*) (Salvatores, 2014) 89
Il ricco, il povero e il maggiordomo ("The rich, the poor and the butler") (Bertacca, 2014) 78
impact of brands in films 77–84
influence on cinema 2
Innocenti, Lambretta 15
International Advertising Festival 91–92
International Basic Economy Corporation (IBEC) 15
Internet 63–64
The invisible boy (*Il ragazzo invisible*) (Salvatores, 2014) 89
Italian Association of Radio and Television Listeners (AIART) 51
Italian cinema, advertising, television, and the state 52–60
Italian Communications Regulatory Authority 3
Italian Communist Party 37
Italian economic miracle 14–16
Italian film production market 68–70
Italianness 9–13
Italian-style comedy (*commedia all'italiana*) 30
Italian television 35; advertising 48–52; anomaly 45–48; monopoly era 18–24

J. Walter Thompson 16

Kezich, Tullio 30

La7 47
La Dolce Vita (Fellini, 1960) 30–31
"Ladri di saponette" (*The Icicle Thief*) (Nichetti, 1989) 52–53
La Grande Bellezza (The Great Beauty) (Sorrentino, 2013) 83–84
Lambretta 15
Lascia o Raddoppia ("Leave it or double it") 19
Lavazza 23
Law No. 244 70
laws: Andreotti law 59; Gasparri law 48; Law No. 244 70; Maccanico law 47; Mammi law 46–47, 54; Reform Law (1975) 45
lead 13
"Leave it or double it" (*Lascia o Raddoppia*) 19
L'Europeo 30
level playing fields, product placement 66–67
lifestyle marketing 62
lifestyle politics 41
literacy 10
logos, product placement 81–82
Lopez, Massimo 44
Loro act 1 (2018) 55
Loro act 2 (2018) 55
lottizzazione 6, 20, 47
lovemarks 62
Luchetti, Daniele 56–57

Maccanico law 47
Made in Italy 12, 28, 69
Maltese, Curzio 56
Mamma RAI 18–24
Mammì law 46–47, 54
Manfredi, Nino 32
Manzi, Alberto 19
Manzoni, Attilio 16
marchetta (sellout) 90
marketing 16; brands and films 71–76; engagement marketing 62; entertainment marketing companies 72–75
marketing politics 37–44
market share of films 29–30, 36

Index   107

Marshall Plan (European Recovery Programme) 11, 13
Martini 83
Mastroianni, Marcello 53
McDormand, Frances 82
media, politics 6
media fragmentation 35
Mediaset 2, 3, 36, 47, 51, 59; product placement 66
Mediterraneo (Salvatores, 1991) 57
Medusa 2, 59
Medusa Film 36
MiBACT (Ministry of Cultural Heritage & Activities and Tourism) 58
Milan, advertising 16
Milano da bere ("Milan to drink") 41
mini-boom 41
Ministry of Cultural Heritage & Activities and Tourism (MiBACT) 58
Montecatini, Moplen 15
Monteleone, F. 50
Moplen 15
Moretti, Nanni 25, 32, 55, 56
Moro, Aldo 17
motorcycles 15
Muddiman, Ashley R. 88
Murdoch, Rupert 47
music channels 42

National Association of Film Industries (ANICA) 26
national film funding 58–60, 65; tax credits 70–71
national identity 9–10
Natta, Giulio 15
Neo-Television 45
network capitalism 73
Nichetti, Maurizio 52, 53
Non è la RAI ("It's not RAI") 45
Non è mai troppo tardi ("It's never too late") 19
Nutella 62

OAPEC (Organization of Arab Petroleum Exporting Countries) 17
Oggi 30
oil embargo (1973) 17

Organization of Arab Petroleum Exporting Countries (OAPEC) 17
Ozpetek, Ferzan 55

P2 ("Propaganda 2") scandal 38
Pacchioni, Federico 25
Paleo-Television 45
panettone 43
Paninari ("sandwichers") 42
Paramount, *Roman Holiday* 29
Partito Democratico della Sinistra (PDS; "Democratic Party of the Left") 54
Pch Media 73
PDS (Partito Democratico della Sinistra) 54
Penn, Sean 81–82
pentapartito 38, 46
Persol 31
Piaggio, Vespa 15, 29
Pitteri, Daniele 16, 24
Placido, Michele 55
plastic 12; Moplen 15
politics: lifestyle politics 41; as marketing 37–44; media and 6
Pontecorvo, Gillo 53
post-war Italy 11; cinema 25–27
print culture 10
Prodi, Romano 47, 68
production companies, product placement 75–76
product placement 31–32, 66–68; agreements for 72; entertainment marketing companies 72–75; film producers 75–76; final cut 82–84; logos 81–82; production budgets 78; scripts 78–79; STET Made in Italy 69
promotional intermediaries 63; entertainment marketing companies 72–75; film producers 75–76
"Propaganda 2" (P2) 38
propaganda newsreel (*cinegiornale*) 28
PSBs (public service broadcasters) 21
pubblicità occulta (surreptitious advertising) 31
public service broadcasters (PSBs) 21
Publitalia 39–40

108   *Index*

QMI, 73
Quo Vado? ("Where am I going?")
  (Nunziante, 2016) 1

Radiocorriere 4, 22
RAI (*Radiotelevisione italiana*,
  "Italian Radio-Television") 2, 3, 6,
  18–21, 36, 44–52, 59, 88; advertising
  "blocks" 50; funding 22; politics 46;
  product placement 66; programming
  decisions 51
RAI Cinema 2
ratings 51
Red Brigades 17
Reding, Viviane 67
reference system, Urbani decree 68–69
Reform Law (1975) 45
regulations, SACIS (*Società per Azioni
  Commerciale Iniziative Spettacolo*)
  21–23
revenues, from advertising 49
riflusso ("backlash") 34
Risorgimento ("Resurgence") 9
Roberts, Kevin 62
Rockefeller, Nelson 15
Roman Holiday (Wyler, 1953) 29

SACIS (*Società per Azioni
  Commerciale Iniziative Spettacolo*)
  21–23
Salvatores, Gabriele 57
"sandwichers" (*Paninari*) 42
Scarpellini, Emanuela 14
Scola, Ettore 25, 53
Scotto Lavina, Enzo 20
scripts, product placement 78–79
Scusate se esisto ("Sorry if I exist") 80
second economic miracle 41
sellout (*marchetta*) 90
service contracts (contratto di
  servizio) 18
Servillo, Toni 84
Shell 21–22
"Single fund for the performing arts"
  (FUS) 58
Sky Italia 47, 51
Socialist Party 38, 39
social media 63
*Società per Azioni Commerciale
  Iniziative Spettacolo* (SACIS) 21–23

Sordi, Alberto 13
Sorlin, Pierre 28
Sorrentino, Paolo 55
"Sorry if I exist" (*Scusate se esisto*) 80
The Space 2
spot advertising 49–50
Stream TV 47
supermarkets 15–16
Supermarkets Italiani SpA 15
surreptitious advertising (*pubblicità
  occulta*) 31
"symbiotic mechanism" 4

tabloid films 30
Tangentopoli ("Bribesgate") 35, 38–39
Taodue 2
Taviani brothers 53
tax credits 70–71
tax shelter 70
Tele+ 47
telecracy 40
Tele Monte Carlo (TMC) 48
telepromozioni (telepromotions) 50
Telescuola ("Teleschool") 19
televendite (teleshopping), 50
television 35; advertising 48–52;
  anomaly 45–48; *Campanile sera*
  ("It's a knockout," 1959-1962) 19;
  DeeJay Television 42; *Il musichiere*
  ("The music maker") 19; *Lascia o
  Raddoppia* ("Leave it or double it")
  19; monopoly era 18–24; *Non è la
  RAI* ("It's not RAI") 45; *Non è mai
  troppo tardi* ("It's never too late")
  19;; *Telescuola* ("Teleschool") 19
television duopoly 44–52
television share of advertising
  expenditures 3
Television Without Frontiers (TVWF),
  46–47, 54, 59, 89
Television Without Frontiers (TVWF)
  Directive, 65–66
terrorism, "Years of Lead" (1969-1980)
  17–18
theatres 35–36
"Them" (*Loro*, 2018) 55
This Must Be the Place (Sorrentino,
  2011) 81–82
TMC (Tele Monte Carlo) 48
Tornatore, Giuseppe 53, 57

Index   109

Toscani, Oliviero 44
trade bodies, advertising agencies 17
TVWF (Television Without Frontiers)
   46–47, 54, 59, 65–66, 89

United States, impact on Italian film
   89–90
UPA (*Utenti Pubblicità Associati*,
   "Association of Advertising
   Users") 17
Urbani decree 68
US films 29
US-made fiction 50
Utenti Pubblicità Associati (UPA,
   "Association of Advertising
   Users") 17

Vacanze di Natale ("Christmas
   holidays") (Vanzina, 1983) 43
Vacanze di Natale a Cortina
   ("Christmas holidays in Cortina")
   (Parenti, 2011) 56
"Vai, paparazzo!" (Wenders, 2015) 31

van Reijmersdal, Eva A. 88
Veltroni, Walter 54
Vespa 15, 29
videocracy 40
Videomusic 42
Virzì, Paolo 55
Visconti, Luchino 25
visual media 10
Vue International 2

Wenders, Wim 31
"Where am I going?" (*Quo Vado?*)
   (Nunziante, 2016) 1
"Wild West" of Italian broadcasting
   history 46
Wojdynski, Bartosz W. 88
Wyler, William 29

"Years of Lead" (1969-1980) 17–18
"You don't interrupt an emotion"
   slogan 53–54

Zeffirelli, Franco 53

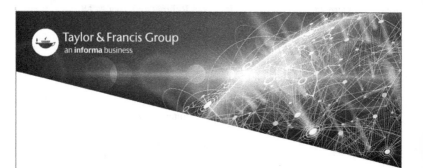

CPSIA information can be obtained
at www.ICGtesting.com
Printed in the USA
BVHW062128020320
573873BV00012B/135